Dear Pastor-

Sorry I haven't church lately. I haven't my way or my faith - Just the old words don't mean what they used to.

Thank you for your shining example of meeting each person right where they live. That is the true meaning of spirit.

Blessings
Kris Binell

ISBN-13: 978-1979624022

ISBN-10: 197962402X

Kris Girrell
1 Meadowbrook Drive
Andover, MA 01810

Cover art:

Art: (first sketch of) "Jacob Wrestling the Angel" by Eugène Delacroix (1798-1863)
http://www.musee-delacroix.fr/spip.php?page=document&id_document=170

Outline

Foreword

Why Wrestling the Angel?

The spiritual life, as I understand it, is ordinary, everyday life lived in an ever-deepening and loving relationship to God and therefore to one's true or healthy self, all people, and the whole of creation. The spiritual life – "Love the Lord your God with all your heart, and with all your soul, and with all your mind, and with all your strength" – and the moral life "Love your neighbor as yourself" – are directly related. The spiritual life, however is prior to the moral life, for we can love our neighbor as God loves us only if first we have experienced that love affair with God. More important, we cannot love God except in response to God's love for us.
This love affair with God is the one and only end of human life. All else is means. [1]

John Westerhoff

Foreword

The challenges of ministry are many, varied and among the most difficult of any role in human service. But willingly heeding and accepting a call often sets one on a deeper more inward journey of spirituality. It is simply not sufficient to have a depth of knowledge of theology and a Bible tucked under one's arm as the sole preparation for a life in ministry. The vocation of ordained ministry (and by extension, one might argue, of lay ministry as well) is one which engages the whole being of the called – body and soul – in its work. And matters of the soul are not "simply" handled or perfunctorily dismissed. If we follow Westerhoff's lead, that our foundational experience in life is the out-pouring of God's love to us, that the "ground of our being," as Tillich calls it, is that source of love, then we are pulled into this "love affair" by the attractive power of love; literally the force which pulls "everything that is toward everything else that is." [2]

Driven by this love, it is the soul (that part of the self that seeks meaning [3]) seeking a deeper understanding of the question of, "What, then, is life and how do I

---

[1] John Westerhoff, *Spiritual Life: The Foundation for Preaching and Teaching* (Louisville, KY: Westminster John Knox Press, 1994), 1.

[2] Paul Tillich, *Love, Power and Justice* (New York: Oxford University Press, 1954), 25.

[3] While theological and philosophical texts are rife with varying definitions of the soul, for the purposes of this discussion, I shall use the simplest definition of soul I can find. In this context, I am

live it?" that defines the spiritual quest. As Thomas Merton put the question, "Who am I, not relative to this or that aspect of my being, but rather who am I *ultimately* before God?"[4] It is not, however, my assumption that every person who experiences a calling chooses that path, nor do I assume that it is only those in the ordained ministry who ask such questions, or even that it is necessary to ask such contemplative questions in order to be on a spiritual path. In fact many may live out their life filled and satisfied with the spirituality of their religion and sustained by the love of God they experience. However, it is also true that many in the field of ministry enter that love relationship trusting that the God of their calling and of their understanding will sustain and support them throughout any trials they may encounter, and when life's realities and challenges prove too challenging, they may be experienced as a challenge to their faith. Among them, many report that, in the process, their spirituality suffers, their formerly sustaining spiritual practices simply dry up, and that at times God seems distant or even non-existent. Their prayers turn from praise and petitions to deep searching questions of "How?" and "Why?" Such a crisis in faith is often referred to as the "dark night of the soul" – a term introduced by the mystic John of the Cross. Not all spiritual journeys lead to an experience of the dark night, but it would appear to me that most experiences of the dark night of the soul result from having started the inward journey toward oneness with the Divine. Whether those called to this inward journey engage in prayer, various forms of meditation, or contemplative practices seems to be irrelevant. It is the act of seeking union with God in one's own manner that launches the journey. This paper proposes to investigate the phenomenon called the dark night of the soul in order to understand its dynamics and the effect it has on spiritual formation and development.

Throughout this thesis, I will use the term contemplative practices to refer various forms of prayer and meditation – knowing full well that there are distinct differences relating to each type of practice. In modern parlance, prayer, meditation and contemplation are often used interchangeably. However, classically meditation was most often used to describe discursive process – focusing on a thought or following a train of logic or reason toward a particular end. In the Christian tradition discursive meditation took one of two forms: Ignatian prayer and *lectio divina*. Ignatian Prayer, developed by Ignatius Loyola in the early 1500s, was developed to help young clerical students identify God's will and follow through on it in their daily lives. It follows a series of focused thoughts or exercises that led the novice through a logical discourse to better understand how to pray and focus the mind.

---

less concerned about debates over the immortality of the soul or its divine nature than I am with the role it may play within the whole of one's personality. Even though mind, self, personality, spirit and soul have at times been used interchangeably in psychological literature, in this discussion I am simply referring to that part of our person with which and through which we seek meaning.

[4] James Finley, *Merton's Palace of Nowhere* (Notre Dame, IN: Ave Maria Press, 1978), 22.

Lectio divina is a practice of reading sacred literature that is a disciplined approach to reflection and acting on a given passage of scripture.

Contemplation, on the other hand, is a process that goes beyond words and is more centered on receptivity and resting in the silence of God. It is this process of contemplation that John of the Cross refers to most frequently as the driver of the inward spiritual journey. But contemplation itself is a practice that is elusive. While there are those whose practice of contemplation leads them to a state of no-self or loss of ego boundaries, for many of us on the path (myself included), contemplation is an exercise in humility and failure. Seeking to still the mind results in a moment of stillness that is quickly replaced by yet another passing thought. Each disruption is in essence a "failure" in practicing contemplation, and those repeated failures teach one a level of humility (that I cannot do this on my own) that is the end point of selfless contemplation. By the same token, each disruption, each passing thought offers what Thomas Merton reportedly called an opportunity to return to opening to God. It achieves the same fruits either way! There seems to be no right way (contemplation, meditation, prayer) to approach the unitive quest and any attempt to "get it right" or do it right" only distances the seeker further from the path of full surrender.

From the beginning of Christianity up through the renaissance, mystics, like the desert monks, Augustine of Hippo, John Duns Scotis, Ignatius Loyola, the Carmelites: Teresa of Avila and John of the Cross, have all focused on contemplation, and contemplative prayer as the processes through which spirit and faith are molded, and as the tools with which one engages in one's spiritual quest. But what actually happens during such contemplative practices? How does contemplation shape and form our faith? Is our faith molded, as Fowler puts it, "as though the great Blacksmith of history, heated [us] in the fires of turmoil and trouble and then hammered [us] into usable shape on the anvil of conflict and struggle?"[5] Is it solely the work of the great Blacksmith or is something very real and identifiable actually happening through contemplation that causes and expedites our movement through the growth and development of faith? Perhaps in some way Fowler's blacksmith shop is what John of the Cross named the dark night of the soul, irrespective of the fact that questioning how our faith evolves seems to have dogged believers since the earliest biblical times.

However the use of the blacksmith metaphor for our spiritual transformation through the dark night of the soul calls up a question of agency. Does God, which for many is the source of love and, as we said, the very force pulling the seeker into the quest for intimacy, cause some painful event so severe that the seeker is launched headlong into the dark night experience? Does a loving God "hammer" us into shape

---

[5] James Fowler, *Stages of Faith: The Psychology of Human Development and the Quest for Meaning* (New York, HarperCollins, 1981), 202.

or is something else happening for which our words and concepts are too feeble to describe? Contrarily, do we naturally encounter "impasses" in living, as Constance FitzGerald calls them,[6] for which our logic and our operating theologies are no match? The blacksmith's fire and anvil may simply be elements of living into a world of chaos wherein we must turn to some sustaining source of love in order to bear the heat of the fire and blows of the hammer. Throughout this thesis I will attempt to articulate the dynamics and the process of spiritual development and transformation through these experiences called the dark night of the soul. Who does what to whom? How is our spiritual life affected in this process and what is actually happening?

Terms and Definitions

The overall methodology of this study will be to fold together an analysis of literature rather strictly limited to theological or pastoral accounts of the dark night experience, and interviews and surveys of a small number of practicing clergy with a focus toward identifying the common threads, difficulties and overall impact of the dark night experience. In each instance, whether literary reference, interviews or direct personal experience, the language used in discussing the dark night of the soul is individually defined and the meaning and intent ascribed to words varies widely. In order to pursue the subject, there are a few of the major concepts and terms that will be used with some frequency throughout the discussion for which a working definition must be laid out. However, therein lies the problem. Highly respected theorists, psychologists and theologians, far more qualified than I have already set forth definitions to these words which conflict with other equally notable sources. That notwithstanding, the nature of the discussion often will delve into issues for which there are no agreed-upon terms or for which those terms that more closely approximate the experience we are attempting to describe have been coopted by others to mean something quite different than what we may be attempting to describe. Therefore the definitions set out in this thesis represent an attempt to codify a common lexicon that most serves the purposes of the thesis rather than what might be found in the standard dictionary.

To begin this discussion it might be helpful to include a few terms that deal with how humans make sense of their world and experiences. I often refer to this as the meaning-making process. How does the human psyche make sense of its world? In the world of John of the Cross (16th century Spain), human psychology was still greatly influenced by the Greek philosophers – Aristotle, Plato and Dionysus.

---

[6] Constance FitzGerald. "Impasse and Dark Night," in *Living with Apocalypse, Spiritual resources for Social Compassion*, Tilden Edwards, ed. (San Francisco: HarperCollins, 1984), 93-116.

Though the Greeks understood the human to be one system, they divided the human person into body and soul, sense and spirit. Though senses could be external or internal, they were distinct from spirit. Thus, when John writes of the senses and the spirit, he probably does so from the perspective of his time.

On the other hand, the average person of today knows far more about human psychology that did the contemporaries of John of the Cross. However, modern psychology understands the human being to be far more complex and multifaceted than even the street knowledge of our peers. According to some personality theories (and here we must turn to C.G. Jung[7] as one of the few in the field who embraced both religion and spirituality within his theoretical framework), we learn that the human psyche is comprised of the conscious and unconscious and that there is even a collective unconscious from which we all borrow in making meaning out of events and perceptions of the world around us. To Jung, the unformed and immature part of our unconscious appears to our conscious ego as negative and ugly. This "shadow" self, as he called it, must be embraced and matured rather than repressed and ignored. The great challenge in according to Jung's model is to face one's shadow, embrace it and integrate it into one's self-knowledge. But the difficult part of that is that the shadow is that which one does not want to admit exists and which one fears others will see. This perspective of the shadow sounds at least to me to be quite similar to what John of the Cross was referring to in his discussions of the "purgations" of the soul (an issue we will discuss in the first chapter). And both of these may differ from what is held as the common or vernacular belief system of today.

Thus we are faced with a problem where there may exist three distinctly differing ways of understanding the terms with which we will explore of the dark night of the soul: the psychology of John of the Cross's era circa the 1500's, modern psychological understanding of human psychology, and perhaps the contemporary or vernacular usage of terms. Irrespective of human psychological theories, it is important to remember that there are aspects of the human that are deeper than personality which lie in an area of mystery. "Buddhists speak of the Buddha nature; Hindus speak of Brahmin and Atman; Hebrews speak of the image of God; Christians speak of the indwelling Holy Spirit; Eastern Christianity speaks of the uncreated energies; mystics of all persuasion speak of the ground of being, the center of the soul, the true self, the void, the emptiness, the cosmic energies."[8] All of these

---

[7] Carl Jung's generally accepted model of human psychological system (see, for example, *Archetypes and the Collective Unconscious*, Vol. 9 of the Collected works of C.G. Jung edited by RFC Hull, 1981) outlines this interrelationship between the levels of consciousness: The conscious ego or persona, the personal unconscious, the collective unconscious and the soul or SELF.

[8] William Johnston, *Mystical Theology, The Science of Love*. (Maryknoll, NY: Orbis Books, 1996), 124.

6

are attempts to name that which lives at the core of our being and which may well influence both meaning-making and spiritual formation.

The following terms and definitions represent a synthesis of modern cognitive psychological perspectives and terms from more recent theological sources used in describing the human experience. Though, as was just said, modern psychology views the human as a complex whole, it may at times be necessary to speak of each element of the person as a separate entity – as if to differentiate it from some other part of the being, knowing that to do so would belie the holistic nature of personhood. There is no place called mind that is devoid of soul or spirit. There is no physical location we can point to as soul, though certainly we could point to brain and heart as places. Yet point we must, if we are to take on the discussion of the dark night of the soul. The various parts of our being function in different and definable ways and these following definitions are simply a way to distinguish those functions from one another.

For purposes of the discussion, let us begin the discussion by considering the self. The **self** in this thesis shall refer to the sum total of an individual's reflective understanding and includes mind, body, ego and all the functions utilized in sense-making, meaning-making, and understanding. Self is a general term that includes all the functions utilized in sense-making and understanding of oneself and of self in relation with all else. Self first comes into being when the child begins to differentiate itself from other entities (other persons, mom, the universe, and at some point God) but, according to C.G. Jung, is not fully manifest until adulthood after a significant number of experiences.

- *Self-consciousness* relies primarily on two differing types of meaning-making functions which, for the sake of this discussion, we shall call the *mind* and the *ego*. Both the mind and the ego are used in processing events, emotions, thoughts, and experiences in an effort to make sense of them.

- *Mind* "employs" intellect, reason, intuition, emotions, the senses and other such tools in an effort to make some sense of relevancy and meaning out of its experience. Mind relegates some information to background (as irrelevant or meaningless), especially if it has no referent or antecedent classification for the experience. Conversely, it elevates other facts and events to foreground or of greater importance.

- *Ego*. At some point in our development, *mind* begins to recognize that the accumulated understandings about itself are in some way consistent and that consistency form begins to dominate how all future self-perceptions are received (and perceived). This formation we shall name the **ego**. From that point on, the mind filters all incoming experiences through the ego in a form of self-fulfilling prophecy ("this is me; this is not me"). While ego could be and often is a term that is interchangeable with self, I tend to side with James Loder's summation of the ego as that which "seeks to equilibrate intrapsychic reality with external reality and so establish a reliable, realistic pattern of defenses and interrelated coping capacities."[9] In other words, ego is the agent of self that takes over the meaning-making process in order to secure and reassure the self that there is some stabile, on-going "reality" of being. Ego is the accumulation of self-referent information collected over time by the mind, which then becomes necessary to preserve as a major cornerstone of meaning making. But both of these were part and parcel of what Jung referred to as the little self.

• On the other side of the discussion of meaning-making, Jung used what he called the big **SELF**. The big SELF is what is generally referred to by soul and spirit. SELF is God within the individual being and in many cases (those with whom I have talked or surveyed in this process) SELF and soul seem synonymous. SELF is the deepest part of our being and that part of the human meaning-making process that seeks meaning in the context of the Divine. Meaning to the soul is understanding the experience as it relates to the greater whole outside of the self – specifically, the Divine. Unlike the mind's functioning, soul is not self-referring – it does not draw on previous personal experiences. Soul, big SELF, is always seeking its context in God.[10] Soul is often discussed as the eternal part of us that was before our conception and continues to exist after our physical death. Hence, because of soul's larger context, it seeks meaning within that larger time and space domain. The rebellious "I am unique and different" of the ego or little self transforms into "my uniqueness is that I am a child of God"[11] when seen by the soul. John of the Cross calls the soul that part of us that is drawn to God and yet at the same time is resting in God. He says the soul is like a stone buried in the ground that continually sinks deeper into the earth, drawn, as it were, by God's gravitational force.[12] In

---

[9] James Loder, *The Transforming Moment* (Colorado Springs: Helmers & Howard, 1989), 70.

[10] Here I'm departing from a strictly Jungian conceptualization to propose that SELF is not just the in-dwelling God but an element of the human meaning making system. However in contrast to the MIND, Soul/SELF's reference point is God.

[11] Much of this definition can be attributed to James Loder in his text, *The Transforming Moment.* Loder's model of the spirit aspect of self includes spirit as the source of creativity and as the drive toward union with God.

[12] Gerald May, *The Dark Night of Soul, A Psychologist Explores the Connection Between Darkness and Spiritual Growth* (San Francisco: HarperCollins Publishing, 2004), 47.

the context of the dark night of the soul, I will use soul and SELF as interchangeable terms along with spirit.

- **Transformation,** as we will be using it in this context, and as opposed to the terms "change" and "development," is defined as a *radical rearrangement or loss* of one's core beliefs, values, meanings and operating assumptions regarding personal existence, the existence and nature of the Divine, and the nature and experience of relatedness/ relationship with a power greater than oneself.[13] Transformation is most often the result of multiple **transformative experiences** and not a single event in time. A transformative experience is one in which the operating assumptions and ways of being break down and give way to a deeper and more complex level of understanding that reveals, in the process, a glimpse of how much further there is to go. Transformative experiences are repeated until the lesson (that this level of understanding will no longer suffice) is learned.

- **God**. Throughout the thesis I will refer to the Divine or to God in various ways. *God*, the Divine, the Lord, YHWH, Higher Power, the Ground of our Being, and other terms used in reference to one's sense of the infinite is an ever-evolving dance of understanding and not-understanding. The term "God," capitalized as a formal name, has been associated more with the concept of the Sky-Father of the ancients However throughout this thesis, what becomes apparent is that through the experience of the dark night of the soul, one's "understanding" of the nature of the Divine and one's relationship with the Divine are in fact what is transformed. God may appear in whatever manner the believer desires or to which s/he can best relate – but most certainly it will no longer be the Sky Father of yore! God – whatever God may be – in God's infinite vastness remains relatively unchanged only our perceptions of God change.

- The phrase *"dark night of the soul,"* a term attributed to St. John of the Cross, refers to a class of experiences characterized by a transition from one previously-perceived type of connectedness with the Divine, through an experience of disconnection, and resolving in a new and different relatedness with the Divine. This is a somewhat broader definition than the sainted mystics, John of the Cross and Teresa of Avila, have described as the dark night experience and somewhat more strictly spiritual experience

---

[13] While my own profession of psychology at times makes reference to both human transformation and to religious development and moral development, I shall largely refrain from attempts to blend the spiritual with the psychological or the sacred with the secular, though clearly at times, there may be a helpful distinction from the secular world of psychology.

than what contemporary writers describe as negative setbacks.[14] The dark night of the soul, as it shall be discussed in this thesis, essentially describes that portion of the spiritual journey, wherein significant changes happen in terms of the individual's experience of and relation to God. My *working assumption* is that there is within each person's story some commonality of process similar to what Saint John of the Cross described. However, while that process may be relatively consistent across individuals, what varies is the precipitating impasse,[15] the nature of how each person deals with it, and where persons can become stuck within that process.

The dark night of the soul often appears as a period of lonely desolation in which spirituality seems to have dried up irrespective of any precipitating event. In a short definition, one might say that the dark night of the soul is "spiritual dryness."[16] For others it is tantamount to a life-and-death struggle, a wrestling match with the very source of life – it is like we are wrestling with God or at least God's emissary as an angel (maybe even the angel of death itself).

However, such experiences are not as uncommon as we might suspect. Not only is scripture rife with references to periods of spiritual dryness, but mystics of all faith traditions from the past to modern day mystics such as Thomas Merton, Constance FitzGerald and Richard Rohr speak openly of them. Beginners, as John of the Cross called those just starting on their spiritual journey, may tend to think of the dark night as a period of spiritual crisis or as times when they feel abandoned by God. Others, like Martin Luther, described his dark night as a "depression" brought on by attacks from the devil, while John Wesley described his "Aldersgate" more like a conversion experience. Moreover, studies of the literature show that these dark nights are often precipitated by external "life" experiences (similar to those described by Fowler[17]) or impasse (as FitzGerald calls it[18]) that color or shape the nature of the

---

[14] Thomas Moore, *Dark Nights of the Soul, A Guide to Finding Your Way Through Life's Ordeals* (New York: Gotham Books, 2004), 1.

[15] Constance FitzGerald describes an impasse as any situation with which our coping mechanisms and our current level of understanding are incapable of dealing for which there is no way out, no way around and no rational way of escaping.

[16] Several writers, most notably, Thomas Moore and Stanislav Grof, have generalized the term to include a wider swath of personal experiences where life itself seems despairing, but for this thesis we will be considering only those experiences that affect the believer's spirituality and the relative impact they have on spirituality.

[17] Fowler's case study examples highlight how each successive stage of spiritual development was catalyzed by a significant life event (See pages 242 and following of James Fowler's, *Stages of Faith*).

individual's dark night, making it difficult to find and classify similarities. As a result, getting a bead on the exact nature of the dark night experience or finding the common language between and among commentaries on the dark night is no simple task. "For this darkness and these trials, both spiritual and temporal, through which happy souls are want to pass in order to be able to attain this high state of perfection, are so numerous and so profound that neither does human knowledge suffice for the understanding of them, nor experiences for the description of them; for only he [sic.] that passes this way can understand it, and even he cannot describe it."[19] In chapter one I will pursue a fuller description of the elements of the dark night experience.

Personal Relevance

This thesis, and the impetus for it, comes partially from my personal experience and my long love/hate relationship with the dark night, and partly from having discussed dark night experiences with ministers and other seminarians along the way. Pursuant to that, I will be including my personal experiences in with the discussions of others and findings of the study. While there are those whose spiritual journey have not been and may never be interrupted by dark nights, and there may be those whose encounter with the dark night is so devastating that they recoil and leave their faith and/or their profession altogether, the bulk of those in ministry with whom I have had such conversations, seem to fall somewhere between the two tails of that distribution, and have had some degree of encounter with the dark night in their relating with God.

Purpose and Goal of the Thesis

My goal in writing this thesis will be two-fold: to discuss in depth the spiritual journey toward intimacy with the Divine through the dark night as experienced by persons of faith[20] (i.e., how does one's *spirituality* evolve or transform as a result of experiencing periods of disconnection or dark nights?), and to delve into how that experience transforms not just the believer but that in which s/he has belief (i.e., how does one's *experience of God* evolve or transform through these dark nights?). It is my hope that in better understanding others' experience of this process we may be able to better guide those who would want to assist ministers and spiritual seekers with their encounters of the dark night of the soul. This could include but is not limited to other ministers, spiritual directors, faculty and church elders.

---

[18] FitzGerald characterizes an impasse as an experience for which there is "no way out, no way around no rational escape from, what imprisons one, [and presents] no possibilities in the situation. In true impasse, every normal manner of acting is brought to a standstill." *Impasse.* 94.

[19] John of the Cross, *Ascent of Mount Carmel*, translated by Allison Peers (New York: Dover Publications, 2008 / 1946), 11.

[20] I have chosen to study this phenomenon as it is perceived by persons in the ministry on the assumption that their vocation often places them on a more pronounced or intentional spiritual path.

Difficulties We Will Confront in Pursuing the Goal

Such an endeavor is fraught with problems from the outset. First, and foremost, as was previously discussed, is the problem of language, beyond the simple establishment of terms and definitions. The world of spirituality lies in a land beyond words. It is, above all else, a knowing without knowing – a feeling or sense at the very best. In fact one of the early mystical texts on the spiritual journey was aptly entitled *The Cloud of Unknowing*. Mystics knew that the original sin of the Adam myth was wanting to know all things – including the knowledge of good and evil. The mystics knew that what must die is that desire to know everything, so that one could come to God innocent of any preconception of who God was and what God expected or wanted from creation.

Putting the ineffable into words automatically diminishes and limits the experience to the common definitions and dualities of vocabulary – that is, labeling some particular thing or experience as "X" connotes that all else is "not-X" and places a false boundary on and around the experience. The language of spiritual experience may be at times contradictory, duplicitous or a complete failure to communicate that which the individual had experienced. Not only do words confine understanding, but each word may have multiple meanings as defined by the history, education, socio-economic background and faith tradition (the construction) of the speaker. As Saint John of the Cross put it, "In order to speak properly of this intuition of naked truth which is conveyed to the understanding, the writer would need God to take his hand and guide his pen; for know, dear reader, that to describe what they are in themselves surpasses all words."[21]

Secondly, descriptions of the Divine, or, more accurately, of the perceptions and experience of the Divine are also beyond words and elusive. For example when Moses was granted the gift of "seeing" the Lord, as God, passed before him, all he could do was bow his head and praise God. And when Job had seen what the Lord showed him of creation, he "fell silent" and refused to speak. But furthermore, as our spiritual journey takes us closer to true encounters with the Divine, our perception of what constitutes the Divine and our experience of God evolve and transform with us. This is not to be confused with some form of "process theology,"[22] but simply an artifact of unveiling the eyes of the seeker – taking off layer after layer so that the perception becomes clearer. However with each successive "insight" the ability to describe what has been revealed becomes more elusive and reveals how much more there is that is not known or perhaps even knowable.

---

[21] John of the Cross, *Ascent*, 194.

[22] Process theologies hold that where we are evolving as a species, and the universe is ever evolving and expanding, so therefore God must also be ever growing evolving and expanding. Taking on this discussion is beyond the scope of this thesis.

And thirdly, seeking to articulate the process through which spiritual directors might assist those on the journey is itself a slippery slope. Often even the most well-intentioned spiritual directors can lead their protégés astray by attempting to describe some element of their own experience or suggesting that the next turn in the path looks a certain way. This not only distorts the perceptions of the seeker who is deep in the throes of their own dark night, but leads them in the wrong direction because of the mimetic aspect of the relationship. As John of the Cross says it, "the spirit of the disciple grows in conformity with that of his spiritual father."[23] And the ego, searching desperately for words to describe and categorize what is happening, latches on to those words and descriptors that may be spoken by the spiritual director, thus altering and shaping the seeker's experience.

However, aware of these cautions, and perhaps in spite them, we will walk cautiously forward in pursuing this quest – a bit like Dorothy and her friends on the road to Oz! Ample warnings abound, like signs along the yellow brick road, for those attempting the trek into the dark night: "The prospect of this wilderness," writes Merton, "is something that so appalls most men [sic] that they refuse to enter upon its burning sands and travel among its rocks."[24] The anonymous author of The Cloud of Unknowing first entreats those who come in possession of the book not to "read it, write or speak about it, nor allow another to do so" unless one deeply believes the recipient of that knowledge is "committed to follow Christ perfectly."[25] Turning to the discussion of contemplation, that first warning is followed up in the next chapter by saying that the reader should "give thanks to God for this calling, so that with the help of God's grace you may stand firm against the subtle assaults of enemies who will harass you from within and without."[26]

Outline and Methods of the Study

This thesis will combine four methods: literature review, a structured survey and interview process and exegetical examination.

The first three chapters are based primarily on literature research. Building on a foundation of writing from Christian mystics and personal/autobiographical commentaries, I will review what others have said about the experience of the dark night of the soul. Mystical writers (e.g., John of the Cross and the author of The Cloud of Unknowing) explore the nature of the dark night experience in terms of training spiritual novices especially on the practice of contemplation and

---

[23] John of the Cross, *Ascent*, 146.

[24] Thomas Merton, *New Seeds of Contemplation* (New York: New Directions Books, 1972, first published by the Abbey of Gethsemane in 1961), 235.

[25] *The Cloud of Unknowing*, translated by William Johnston (New York: Doubleday Image Books, 1973), 35.

[26] *The Cloud of Unknowing*, 37.

contemplative prayer. Their instruction outlines the stages and elements of spiritual development, being careful not to imply steps or stages, which deal with spiritual dryness and the problems of attachment to certain concretized beliefs and values. Chapter two presents support of my central thesis that the experience of the dark night of the soul is a frequently occurring and perhaps commonplace element of the spiritual journey through a look into several biblical characters and stories. While many look to the Book of Job or the Psalms as the ultimate dark night of the soul accounts in the Bible, I contend (as do John of the Cross and others) that the Bible is filled with accounts of the struggle to seek union with God, to maintain a connection with God, the pain and anguish that fills a person when that is lost, and the incredible transformation that occurs as a result. Consider for example the stories of Abraham, Joseph, Jacob, Elijah, David, Job, the Psalmists, Isaiah, Jeremiah, Jonah, and in the New Testament, Jesus, Peter, and Paul, all of whom struggle through the presence/absence cycles of spiritual connectivity; and those are just the main characters. In fact the title for this thesis comes from one of those great dark nights of the ancient scriptures: Jacob's night-long wrestling match with the angel (or some avatar of God) that altered his life forever.

Chapter three provides a counterpoint to the structures of the mystics and biblical writers, through three personal narratives; stories from ministers and theologians who have personally experienced the dark night of the soul (though not specifically naming as such). We look at these narratives more to see if contemporary spiritual persons experience the dark night in similar ways to those described by the mystics. These stories provide us with an inside-out look at what it feels like to be in the throes of the spiritual despairing today, and give us a sense of just how widely varied descriptions of the dark night experience can be. Like the dream of Jacob, our encounters in the night often grab us and engage us in what feels like a life-and-death struggle or what Richard Rohr calls "the Divine Ambush." The bulk of contemporary literature on the dark night of the soul consists of personal narratives that are as varied as the number of authors writing them. While these narratives provide only a little in the way of understanding the process, a look across several of them begins to show some signs of patterning and provide a window into the human experience. This chapter is a brief summary of three such novels (Armstrong, *The Spiral Staircase*; Weems, *Listening for God*; Mother Teresa, *Come Be My Light*) that are provided as background. Added to these, I will also include a short description from my own experiences with the dark nights of my spiritual journey.

Chapter four is based on interview and survey data collected from 82 protestant ministers.[27] [28] Hoping to gather more information from contemporary ministers, a structured questionnaire combining open response, forced choice and multiple choice items was administered to a target population of ministers, predominately in two protestant denominations with which I am most connected (UMC and ELCA along with a small handful of other acquaintances).[29] Because of the nature of self-identified and anecdotal data, no attempt was made to use statistically sound sampling techniques or to analyze the data for statistical relevance. The purpose of the questionnaire was: 1) to garner a larger sample of personal narratives of what precipitated the dark night, 2) to see how that experience was perceived, 3) to ascertain what sustained the believer during the experience and 4) to identify what changed as a result of the experience. These answers and data will help to inform a descriptive classification system (in Chapter 5) as evidence of how the dark night experience may be perceived at different stages of faith (or what I shall later call "operational states").

Chapter 5 deals more with the after-effects of the dark night experience. Coming out of the dark night of the soul, one is forever changed in many ways – in truth, one is spiritually transformed. In the story of Jacob, the protagonist is wounded by the touch of the angel (or God) and, as the story goes, is both renamed as a sign of his transformation and walks with a limp from that point on. Likewise in our own dark night experiences, we are wounded as well. From my experience, it appears as though the wound is one that attacks our area of greatest strength, seemingly because that is where we place our greatest personal pride, ownership, and attachment. As the data in chapter three suggest, this happens in a number of different ways depending

---

[27] Approval to conduct and use this type of research with human subjects has been granted the HSR Subcommittee at ANTS.

[28] Surveys were solicited from 91 practicing ministers and rabbis (the latter being asked purely as a result of several interesting conversations with Rabbis about the dark night). For the purposes of the paper those 9 rabbis were not included leaving 82 respondents of which 11 said they had never had a dark night experience. The chapter deals with the responses of the remaining 71 ministers responding positively to the dark night question.

[29] These two populations were selected for convenience and expediency and, because of that non-randomized sampling process, not intended to provide any statistical relevance. The effort is simply to gain a greater than "N=1" narrative as a basis of comparison. As I am a practicing Lutheran and have many acquaintances within the Lutheran denomination, I solicited the assistance of James Hazelwood Bishop of the ELCA New England Synod to contact as many Lutheran ministers as I could beyond my immediate circle. My daughter, Reverend Rebecca Girrell, is an ordained minister and Elder of the United Methodist Church and a representative to the World, National and Northeast Jurisdictional conferences. With her assistance, I was able to access a fairly large number of UMC ministers. (It should be noted that both Luther and Wesley experienced and wrote about their dark nights of the soul, some of which made its way into their respective doctrines). One hundred ministers and rabbis were contacted with a net return of 92 surveys.

on the individual's life experience and age. Paul (the former Saul of Tarsus), who was a reformed persecutor of followers of "the way," spoke several times of the "thorn in his flesh" and the ailment in his side that tormented and persecuted him, continually reminding him of his humility and keeping him from "exalting" himself.[30] Nonetheless, as a result of the dark night experiences we are forever changed: Spiritually, beliefs that were once rigid and firmly held shift to being far more tentatively held.[31] Interpersonally, perceptions of others' beliefs and of their struggles are seen with deeper compassion whether understood or not.[32] Theologically, one's understanding of God shifts significantly, as the former experiences and ideas are replaced with new ones.[33] This progressive hermeneutic, as it were, will be summarized in a chart in chapter 4 that maps the changing structure of one's core beliefs across a gradient of what I call "operational states" of spirituality. Through it all, the believer emerges with a renewed hopefulness based not in his or her own needs and desires but on the trust that God is and has been "there" all along.[34] Throughout the process one gains humility and gentleness about speaking of one's experiences, careful not to assert the "truth" of one's own experiences or their existence as either greater/better than or even different from others' experiences.

In chapter six I will briefly outline a foundational theology[35] - a theology of the dark night – that I believe expresses the results of transformation described thus far and provides a context for understanding the changes that occur in the dark night experience.

Limitations of the study

The thesis concludes in the afterword with several suggestions for further research, for the publication of a resource list for spiritual seekers and the directors

---

[30] ANTS professor Simon Lee contends that this may have been his eyesight which, as a result of the blinding light, became poorer as he aged.

[31] Thomas Merton, *New Seeds of Contemplation* (New York: New Directions Books, 1961)

[32] James Loder, *The Logic of the Spirit* (San Francisco: Jossey-Bass, 1998).

[33] James Fowler. *Stages of Faith* (New York: HarperCollins, 1981).

[34] Richard Rohr. *The Naked Now* (New York: Crossroads Publishing, 2009).

[35] My theological stand is rooted in the writings of Paul Tillich and Teilhard de Chardin (See chapter 6). Tillich described God as the ground of our being, the source of all life. His concept of God's continual out-pouring of love as the force which draws us together in relationship with others and with God disallows a system wherein God is the agent of pain and suffering, but is one that totally accounts for the pull forward into the spiritual quest for connection. Power, on the other hand, says Tillich, is that inner drive which desires to manifest itself as different and unique. Teilhard modifies the creation narrative and thus the core of Christology through his understanding of science and evolution. However both see God in, through and under the whole of creation and refer to Christ not as a personage but as the Divine blueprint of creation.

who assist them, and for possible study themes for others following this path. A partial resource list will be included. Though this will be discussed further in the afterword, it should be noted at the outset that there are indeed several limitations to this study. First of all, this thesis is limited to a point of view of the author. As one intimately familiar with the dark night I may have selected others' stories and select references that fit with my perception and support my main thesis. By definition, then, it has a natural bias meant to tell the story as I see it. In truth, I can do nothing other than to see through my own eyes and seek evidence that supports that perception. While I contend that the others whose works I cite and whose experiences I describe are supportive of that point of view, I fully realize that the spiritual journey is so personal and individually defined that no one point of view could hold them all.

The study itself (that is, the survey data collected) is limited to a very small subset of professional clergy and at that, those who were included in the survey were neither screened nor sampled randomly. As such no valid generalizations can be made of the observations and anecdotal information collected. Data in this study can only be used in describing those who were included in it.

On a larger perspective, this thesis is focused not on all encounters of the dark night, but rather only on those whose career is directly related to spirituality. As Renita Weems puts it, it is one thing for any individual to experience a crisis in their faith but for a minister to realize that much of the journey is stumbling and falling in the dark, seems to be an admission of failure.[36] Furthermore, rather than adhering to a strict definition of the dark night of the soul as described by John of the Cross, I deviate from that purist point of view and follow a more generic classification of dark night along the lines of what Constance FitzGerald calls "Impasse." That notwithstanding, I will not include more personal crises that have little or nothing to do with one's spirituality as falling within the realm of the dark night of the soul despite contentions by well-respected psychologists that they constitute spiritual emergencies or dark night-like crises.[37] This study is mostly concerned with the inward spiritual journey and how it evolves over time and repeated experiences of the dark night.

Lastly, though this work may apply to several classes of people – seminarians, ministers, and others in various walks of faith and religious traditions– the ideas put forth in this thesis are speculative, theoretical and not validated. The classification system explained in the fifth chapter in particular is hypothetical and

---

[36] Renita Weems, *Listening for God: A Minister's Journey Through Silence and Doubt* (New York: Touchstone/Simon & Schuster, 1999), 25.

[37] Stansilav Grof and Christina Grof, *The Stormy Search for the Self, a guide to personal growth through transformational crisis* (Los Angeles: Jeremy Tarcher, Inc, 1990), 47.

not the result either of a scientific or statistical observation. These all may be suggested as lines of further study.

Chapter One

**When Things Go Bump In The Night:
The Process and Description of the Dark Night**

I would, then, that I could convince spiritual persons that this road to God consists not in multiplicity of meditations nor in any ways nor methods of sides, nor in consolations, although these things may be in their own way necessary to beginners, but that it consists only in the one thing that is needful, which is the ability to deny oneself truly, giving oneself up to suffering for Christ's sake, and to total annihilation. And if the soul be found wanting in this exercise, which is the sum and root of the virtues, all its other methods are so much wondering about in a maze, and profiting not at all, although its meditations and communications may be as lofty as those of the angels.[38]

John of the Cross

Describing the Dark Night of the Soul

The noted father of experimental psychology, B. F. Skinner, is reported to have once quipped, "Nature never conducted a pure experiment." The same may be true of our experience of the dark night. While monastics, from the time of the desert monks, may have had the luxury of withdrawing from the business and busyness of the world in order to conduct "pure" experiments of their journey of spirituality, post-modern society often does not afford us such luxuries. The description of the dark night process John of the Cross provides for us may well be an accurate description – and certainly warrants discussion here – but it may become less applicable or more difficult to use as a template in the busy, multimedia-infused lives of today's clerics. In this chapter I aim to provide a classical description of the dark night of the soul as described by John of the Cross. However I will be highlighting those elements that I believe are most relevant to understanding the cause and effect of the dark night and that I believe are most critical in understanding the transformation that is the on-going effect on the believer as it may occur today. In doing so I may have to adopt a broader understanding of the dark night, but it should be enough to guide the discussion if we are to understand the experiences of our sisters and brothers of today who may still be in the throes of the dark night passage.

Who Was John of the Cross?

Though accounts of spiritual despair and spiritual transformation exist before him, the term "dark night of the soul" is generally attributed to John of the

---

[38] John of the Cross. *Ascent*, 91.

Cross, a Spanish Carmelite monk in the second half of the 16th century. Saint John of the Cross's writings[39] are considered to be among the most detailed of the texts describing the inward spiritual journey to union with the Divine. John of the Cross wrote from a deep personal experience of his calling and of his encounters with God. Perhaps because of the authentic (personal) truth of his experience, but certainly complicated by joining a purist faction of the Carmelites led by Teresa of Jesus (later to be known as Teresa of Avila) whom he met in his twenties, he was seized by the ruling class of the church and imprisoned for his beliefs that the Order ought to be reformed – a belief that the Prior General took as an insult. During the nine months of his imprisonment, he was kept in solitary confinement and beaten daily by those whom he most respected. It was during this period of confinement and torture that John of the Cross began writing his poetic descriptions of his faith journey. And though he never mentions the pain of his beatings and confinement, it was no doubt the catalyst that launched him into his own exploration of the dark night of the soul.

After his release, John of the Cross traveled throughout Spain teaching, at times partnering with Teresa of Jesus on the lessons of the spiritual journey, and writing his poetry and the explanations of it for the growing numbers of followers. John was elected the Vicar of the region and founded his first monastery in Duruelo, changing his name to John of the Cross. His teachings and spirituality were so great that he went on to found several other monasteries and to become the spiritual director to his mentor Teresa. John of the Cross's understanding of spiritual transformation through the dark night of the soul led to his being recognized as the primary authority on understanding the dark night.

But he warns us that this understanding does not come easily. Perhaps that is why the bulk of his writing – certainly in the *Ascent of Mount Carmel* – concerns what this isn't or what one must let go of in the pursuit of God. "To enter on this road is to leave the road; or, to express it better, it is to pass on to the goal and to leave one's own way, and to enter upon that which has no Way, which is God."[40] Often John of the Cross's writing appears to the novice as apophatic theology, but it is more a result of understanding that anything one wishes to describe, such as love, cannot fit into a nice neat box or glib definition. As beginners, John of the Cross says, we start this journey with an extremely

---

[39] John of the Cross wrote throughout his life and compiled those writings into four major works: *The Dark Night of the Soul, Spiritual Canticle, Ascent of Mount Carmel* and *The Living Flame of Love*. Though *The Dark Night of the Soul* speaks directly to our topic, its poetic and allusive structure is more of a commentary along the path, whereas *Ascent of Mount Carmel* is more straight-forward and instructive, and provides more structure to understanding the process of entering and passing through the dark night.

[40] John of the Cross, *Ascent*, 76.

limited understanding of what God is, and it is that dim image in a fogged mirror as Paul told the Corinthians, which no longer serves us, that must be left behind.

Classical mystical traditions often talk of the three-fold way: The way of beginners, the way of proficients and the way of perfection or of mastery.[41] Likewise in Christian mystical tradition, masters like Ignatius Loyola, Thomas Aquinas, and John of the Cross discussed the *via purgativa, via illuminativa* and *via unitiva.* The way of beginners was seen as the purgation of impurities (that which could get in the way of the journey). The *via purgative* begins with a conversion of the heart; shunning sin (that which turns us away from God) to turn toward God. Spiritually this is seen as a turning away from the outward world of glamour and attachments (things) to turn inward to seek the purity of the in-dwelling God. The way of illumination (*via illuminativa*) was seen not as a path of intellectual enlightenment but rather of seeing in the darkness, or the path of unknowing. It is only in the darkness that we can be illuminated by the light. And the way to unity with the Divine, rather than the way of intellectualism as the name might suggest, is seen as a way of surrendering one's imperfection to the perfect love of the Divine. God alone is the perfect expression of love, but being created in the image of God, our loving is a reflection of that perfect loving, which ultimately places the seeker of God on the *via unitiva.*

And with that, let us begin to walk these three paths that lead into and through the dark night of the soul. John of the Cross's explanation of the dark night experience breaks it into two major processes: the dark night of the senses and the dark night of the spirit. The dark night of the senses had to do with how one perceives life, i.e., through the senses. Thus the dark night of the senses had to do with how the beginner perceived his/her world but more importantly how those perceptions (senses) were perceived as naturally pleasing to the person. The spirit, on the other hand, was the domain of God and the Holy Spirit. Therefore his discussion of the dark night of the spirit focused on changes in the perception of how God and the Holy Spirit were experienced by the believer.

These two arenas are each broken further into subprocesses that John called "active" and "passive" nights. The active night consists in what the soul can do for itself and in what the individual does in initiating the journey (matters of will and disciplines like contemplative prayer). The passive way is that wherein the soul does nothing from its intention but rather it is where God "works mysteriously in the soul."[42] Active nights are those times where the individual is aware of participation in life and in the spiritual journey and passive dark nights are where it seems as though God is invisibly working inside us,

---

[41] Johnston, *Mystical Theology,* 142 ff.
[42] John of the Cross, *Ascent,* 59.

irrespective of our participation or even our awareness. The former functions to free us from our attachments to things that gratify our "senses" while the latter breaks down and redefines our rigid beliefs and ways of thinking[43].

In both, however, there is much associated pain and grief. Mapping these two descriptive elements together produces in essence a two-by-two grid that may look something like this:

	Senses	Spirit
Active	**Action**: Through my effort I have caused things to happen that are now being taken away. **Pain**: Loss of passion and zest for life, disinterest in spiritual practices that now seem useless and stupid.	**Action**: Through prayer and spiritual practices, I have been in relationship with my God. **Pain**: Loss of connectivity; prayers and worship dry up and are fruitless
Passive	**Action**: Unconditional love destroys ego and logic systems and confusion, "spiritual madness," and terror set in. **Pain**: God makes no sense at all. Dualistic cause and effect are replaced with non-dual[44], holistic awareness	**Action**: We are being claimed by God through no effort of our own. God moves from external relationship to in-dwelling partnership. **Pain**: Surrender and contemplation reveal that I am nothing myself but everything in God.

Figure 1. Aspects of the Dark Night of the Soul

However, this diagram would appear to separate the night of the senses from the night of the spirit and active nights from passive. This is a gross oversimplification of the dark night, in order that we might be able to better describe all of what is going on. In actuality (or at least in my own experience and according to my read of John of the Cross) it is nothing like that. Sense and

---

[43] May, *The Dark Night*, 80.

[44] The reference to "non-dual" thinking as contrasted with holistic thinking or oneness is attributable to Fr. Richard Rohr, his many writings and spiritual guidance as a personal teacher. Rohr distinguishes non-dualism as simply holding the tension of "both-and" where our Western minds have been accustomed to seeking dualistic opposites and exclusive "rightness" of one side over the other.

spirit are simply the names of the aspects of the soul as described by Greek philosophy (which still influenced the thinking of most philosophers and theologians of the sixteenth century). The night of the senses and the night of the spirit are so intertwined that it is hard at times to know what or which is happening. Though John of the Cross does at times refer to the night of the spirit as the "second night" it is only in distinguishing it from the previously described night of the senses. Other translations call the night of the spirit the "other night."[45] Likewise the active and passive processes, that is, our attempts to seek relationship with God and what might appear as love (God) acting on us, are simultaneous and often intertwined as well. John of the Cross only uses this language to provide beginners with a way to describe or put words to the aspects of the dark night. Gerard May says that the unfortunate truth about the dark night experience is that most people are aware only of John's poetic description of the active night and that few actually understand the aspects of the passive nights.[46] Scripturally, we see an example of this understanding (or lack thereof) in the Book of Job. Most readers are aware of Job's physical suffering (senses) and mental anguish (spirit) as well as his active role in the discourse, but often most fail to see the places where the passive night might be inferred from what transpires and is unwritten between the latter chapters.[47] That having been said, there is a certain sequential nature to the two nights in that one must necessarily have done some inner work of the nature of the night of the senses in order to be aware of the inner work of the night of the spirit. But to presuppose that God will wait for the "green light" to begin the spiritual work or that the seeker can of his/her own will or volition cause God to do anything, erroneously leads to the belief that the two nights are or must be sequential.

John of the Cross informs us that we can identify the onset of the dark night of the soul by the appearance of three signs: 1) the dryness and impotence of our spiritual practices, 2) the lack of desire for the old ways, and 3) a simple desire to love God.[48] Each of these three signs marks the onset of the dark night of the soul and therefore both the dark night of the senses as well as the dark night of the spirit.

Spiritual dryness

---

[45] The authoritative translation of John of the Cross is by Alison Peers. However Gerald May and other translations such as recently by Mirabai Starr, read the original Spanish each slightly differently.

[46] May, *Dark Night*, 85.

[47] I will return to Job as well as other biblical references to the dark night experience in a later chapter.

[48] May, *Dark Night*, 136-142.

Psychologist and spiritual teacher James Finley describes John of the Cross's first section on the "way of beginners" as the "process of ego being illuminated by faith."[49] One's belief is an idea about God; a finite idea about the infinite. But beliefs describe only a small part of that infinite which is God. It is our felt sense of God's abiding presence in our lives. "Knowledge that one is loved is not just theory. It is real, lived experience, for the mystical life begins when a blind stirring of love (the terminology is from *The Cloud*) rises in the heart."[50] But the ego mistakes the feeling of continual and abiding divine presence *as* God. Along the way, the desire to know God and the faith in or of God begins to illuminate that mistaken identification as folly. As the beginner experiences more of God's presence, the finiteness of one's belief system, and the fact that God cannot be limited by thoughts of God, is exposed and eliminated.[51] In this way both the fabrications of the little self (ego) are dismantled and the little self is exposed as just another of the mind's fabrications which must also be destroyed by the fire of absolute love. The absoluteness of love – that is of God – does not however annihilate our identity (in the process of annihilating little self) but rather reveals the ultimate source of our identity in love (that is, SELF). Egoic self is exposed as lacking understanding and beliefs about God, or love, when juxtaposed against the power of unfathomable love. The senses experience God but just as quickly lose their grasp on anything that the ego might utilize in claiming knowledge and "the sense of presence gives way to a sense of absence."[52] This presence/absence shift is a part of what John of the Cross described in the dark night of the senses. And almost spontaneously this sensual dark night cascades into a spiritual dark night. The beginner necessarily loses the strength of his/her belief system as each belief, each finite (known) idea of the infinite, is broken apart in the presence of infinite love. The experience the beginner has of this is a sense of a loss of faith. Spirituality loses its luster. What once was a source of comfort becomes dry and senseless.

As we continually confront the finite images of God with an experience of, or at least the glimpse of a more infinite God, through God's infinite loving of us, it creates a continual and on-going inner critique of our feeble images of God. At first these critiques feel as though they may come from elsewhere; as though God is critiquing us and our thoughts. The beginner perceives God as the

---

[49] James Finley, *The Divine Ambush*, lecture delivered for the Center for Action and Contemplation, Santa Fe, NM, April 18-20, 2013.

[50] Johnston, *Mystical Theology*, 175.

[51] For me and for my personal dark night, this was apparent in a sense that there was no place I could hide from God or from God's call.

[52] Johnston, *Mystical Theology*, 176.

agent of change in spirituality, and, much like Job, desires to stand her/his ground and shout at God for causing the pain and suffering. But what is really happening is that further and deeper contemplation of the mysterious causes a purification of oneself which produces what Michael Buckley calls a "progressive hermeneutic" of the nature of God.[53] Each successive experience of God reveals more of the nature of God and at the same time a greater awareness of how little one really knows of God. "Since God does not communicate through the senses or through some discursive analytical thought,"[54] the ego has nothing to grab hold of; the senses are devoid of information and appear to dry up. The words of God, and the words about God, the special prayers and phrases of one's spiritual tradition, all become meaningless and, in losing their meaning, become powerless and dry. Darkness falls on both the senses and on the spiritual side of life. Simply put, "darkness is the place where egoism dies and true unselfish love for the 'other' is set free."[55]

Lacking desire for the old ways

Through this progressive hermeneutic, the beginner catches occasional glimpses of how deep, how vast and how penetrating God's love may be. And coming to the understanding that this was not understood previously, beginners become skeptical of spiritual practices that had served them in the past. Quite simply the old Sunday School religion becomes incapable of carrying or sustaining the beginner in this deeper understanding. The beginner must come to a realization that s/he lacks the process skills to come to a deeper understanding of the infinite. We can no longer trust our senses to "make sense" out of what is happening. We can no longer trust our intellect to comprehend what is happening nor can it comprehend the brief glimpses of God's fullness. While "sciences can be acquired by the light of the understanding," writes John of the Cross, "the science that is of faith is acquired without the illumination of the understanding."[56] Like mythical Adam and Eve, our desire to know, to eat of the fruit of the tree of knowing, not only gets in the way, it pushes us further from God. We perceive the nakedness of this truth and are ashamed of what we have done to distance ourselves from the source of all life, love and understanding.

At this point beginners lose trust in the old methods of perceiving and the old spiritual practices. It becomes clear "that faith is a dark night to the soul" and

---

[53] Michael J. Buckley, unpublished paper for the Jesuit School of Theology in Berkeley, "Atheism and Contemplation" p. 694 web, http://www.ts.mu.edu/readers/content/pdf/40/40.4/40.4.2.pdf

[54] FitzGerald. *Impasse*, 99.

[55] FitzGerald. *Impasse*, 101.

[56] John of the Cross, *Ascent*, 72.

that it must be "in darkness as to its own [false] light, so that it may allow itself to be guided by faith to this high goal of union."[57] If this sounds like double-talk from John of the Cross, it is. The process of faith, seeking union with God, remains the same but the tools and techniques become less clear. What once was a cause-and-effect spiritual process (e.g., when I pray, I experience God's support and love) is exposed as a lie of the ego. The little self, that part of us that seeks to make sense of things (and therefore *use* those things), has laid claim to causality. The shift that must occur is in dropping the belief that relationship with the Divine can be achieved in any way at all by willfulness.

> At the deepest levels of the night, in a way that one could not have imagined it could happen, one sees the withdrawal of all one has been certain of and depended upon for reassurance and affirmation… All supports seem to fail one and only the experience of emptiness, confusion, isolation, weakness, loneliness and abandonment remain. In this frantic search for reassurance, one wonders if anyone – friend, spouse or God – is really 'for me,' is trustworthy. But no answer is given to the question.[58]

Essentially what FitzGerald is saying is that even one's credo, the understanding of one's faith and religion as it has been, even one's view of scripture, fails and creates more confusion or seems to fall into emptiness and meaninglessness. The old ways hold no meaning and no potential for salvation. As both our tools of sensation and meaning-making, and our experience of spirituality break down, we are left with only questions and no answers. And ultimately, though much further on in the process, even the questions fall away as we stand, slack-jawed, in awe of the presence and overwhelming nature of the love of God.

Through all of this, John of the Cross is careful not to ascribe agency to God but rather tells the beginner that the ends and the means are the same - love. If we hold fast to the belief that God is love, then the way to God is simply (though at this point in the journey, not so simply) a desire to love God, which John of the Cross says is the third sign.

Desire to love God

---

[57] John of the Cross, *Ascent.* 74. Note: the inserted word "false" is mine.

[58] FitzGerald, *Impasse*, 103-104.

This, according to John of the Cross, is the proverbial sticky wicket! The beginner is continually tripped up by the mind's need to understand and make sense of process tools and to claim agency in the spiritual journey.

> Passing beyond all that which can be known and understood, both spiritually and naturally, the soul will desire with all desire to come to that which in this life cannot be known, neither can enter into its heart. And leaving behind all that it experiences and feels, both temporally and spiritually, and all that it is able to experience and feel in this life, it will desire with all desire to come to that which surpasses all feeling and experience. And in order to be free and void to that end, it must in no wise lay hold upon that which it receives, even spiritually or sensually, within itself.[59]

To love as God loves, as Roberta Bondi describes it, seems at first a quest to seek perfection in loving. God is the ultimate expression of love, thinks the little self, I therefore must seek to be perfect in my loving as well. But Bondi tells us that love is achieved not through knowing and seeking perfection but by "unknowing." She equates this unknown way of love to the experience a parent has of her child. There is a moment parents come to where they suddenly realize that though they intimately know their children, their children will have lives that are completely unknown by their parents – that children are not simply an extension of their parents' aspirations and expectations. Likewise, we can place no expectations on the love of God or our loving of God.[60]

In moving to a pure desire to love God, beginners move from a conceptual cataphatic theology (naming God and God's qualities) to an apophatic theology of processes. This process is no longer about getting it right or trying to figure things out. Rather this theology of processes is one that is engaged in for the pure sake of the experience, knowing that thought and descriptions at this point can only come from the experience itself.[61] Each experience registers on the mind as a known instance and must immediately be let go of as something of the former way of being. One comes to understand that God is not that which was just experienced but was that which was behind the experience. The mind is no longer permitted to make statements about God and must surrender to unknowing and yet experiencing. "The soul must be stripped of all things created and of its own actions and abilities, so that when all that is

---

[59] John of the Cross, *Ascent*, 76-77

[60] Roberta Bondi, *To Love as God Loves: Conversations With the Early Church* (Philadelphia: Fortress Press, 1987), 96-97.

[61] Buckley, *Atheism*, 690.

unlike God and unconformed to him it is cast out, the soul may receive the likeness of God.[62],

This presents us with a difficult dilemma. The cosmic joke behind the quest of spirituality is that we cannot – that is, our conscious minds cannot – tolerate being loved unconditionally in our brokenness. While we begin to understand unconditional love as God's nature, we simultaneously become increasingly aware of our own finiteness and brokenness in what we can and cannot do. And the really sad part of this state is that we give more authority to our broken condition than to God's infinite capacity for unconditional love.[63] The great "aha" in the process is the discovery of God's unconditional love for us despite our brokenness. The eschatology of the dark night is that God is, in fact, and in being, and in action, total and unconditional love. But love here is both the source and the action, both noun and verb, both process and endpoint, and at the same time totally beyond comprehension.

Ironically, it is precisely in being broken, poor and powerless that we can be broken open to allow God's loving in. At this point in the dark night experience one comes to the realization of nothing – no belief, no theology, no assurance – there simply is nothing but faith to which one can cling, and this realization triggers in most a "deep, silent, overpowering panic."[64] For some, however, this comes as a feeling of "no faith" instead of a feeling of "nothing but faith." The seeker wonders, "how can I hold on to my faith or use my faith as any sort of anchor when all else of my being is broken and powerless? Would it not then follow that my faith itself is broken?" Though, to be certain the experiences of "no faith" and "nothing but faith" are distinctly different, the net effect of being shaken deeply to the core leads both to an impasse of no return. It is as desolate and isolated a place as the soul can experience. This is the last vestige of ego's attempt to have power and when that gets dashed to the ground, when we finally give way to our powerlessness, John of the Cross tells us, we move into a world of self-esteem, affirmation, compassion and solidarity with all creation. Only such an experience, says FitzGerald, has the power to change "'I' into 'we' enabling us to say, 'we poor,' 'we oppressed,' 'we exploited.' The poor are objects until we are poor, too."[65] We are separate from all of humanity (a fiction created by our ego-driven individuation process) until our perception of uniqueness and of having some favored state is broken and destroyed. What we learn is that unless we are stripped of our egoic belief of difference, and unless

---

[62] John of the Cross, *Ascent*, 80.

[63] Finley, CAC lecture.

[64] FitzGerald, *Impasse*, 104.

[65] FitzGerald, *Impasse*, 104.

we are humbled by this devastating pain, we can never really identify with all of humanity which includes the poor, oppressed, and outcast.

Under deeper examination what we see is how this failure takes place. Prayer fails because it consists of finite words addressing a finite concept of the infinite love of God. We all learned of the world as children do, through our senses – that is, words mean nothing until/unless there is an experience to make sense of it. Much of our world of understanding is based on having an antecedent sensual/physical experience. Likewise the concepts we associate with God are simply concepts that we have based on the experiences of the touches of God's love. When prayer fails it sets off a cascade of other sense-based failures. John of the Cross says that we lose our taste, and ultimately our lust for life itself. What we have to realize as "powerless" is that our world of words and concepts, based mostly in our childhood learning experiences, are powerless in describing that which is no longer understood, nor understandable. In coming to that powerlessness, we are stripped of our illusion of separateness and become one with others and the world around us.[66]

Welcome to the dark night of the soul.

The pain and suffering associated with this discovered powerlessness of our ego is often so deep and physical that it can be immobilizing. Teresa of Avila described the pain as being pierced with a flaming dagger:

> I saw in his hands a large golden dart in at the end of the iron tip there appeared to be a little fire. It seemed to me this angel plunged the dart several times into my heart and it reached deep within me. When he drew it out I thought he was carrying off with him the deepest part of me; and he left me all on fire with a great love of God. The pain was so great that it made me moan, and the sweetness that this greatest pain caused in me was so superabundant that there is no desire capable of taking it away; nor is the soul content with less than God.[67]

When, in this suffering, we pray for relief, it slowly dawns on us that even Jesus was not spared from suffering. We begin to realize that there is no

---

[66] While this description may sound like some linear, step-wise progression, it is anything but linear. The linearity of my description is an attempt to codify some elements of the process of the dark night which, experientially, can only be described with words like "whirlwind," "insanity," "chaos," and "being in the vortex." Throughout the paper, it is necessary to adopt a language of linearity. Later, in my analysis of the changes in operating logic that occur through the dark night of the soul (Chapter 5), I actually delineate what would appear to be steps or stages, I will nonetheless contend that it is as non-linear and confusing a process as any one might experience in life.

[67] Teresa of Avila, *Interior Castle* (Translation by Allison Peers. Originally published by New York: Sheed & Ward, 1946.) Mineola, NY: Dover Publications, 1946, 29.

place we can go to in this finite world where suffering cannot reach us and that there are no amount of words or concepts or theologies that can stop the suffering we feel and see around us. It is only at that point, where one fully understands that trying to overcome suffering by *understanding* it is doomed to fail miserably and completely, that one finally understands the full extent of our personal (cognitive) powerlessness. It is at this darkest point of nothingness that, if one has fully let go of trying to "get" it, to figure it out, to pray it away, at the point where one is devoid of words and thoughts and senses, one suddenly realizes or feels a strange warmth inside. It may be small at first, inexplicable, incomprehensible and yet growing. It is a deeper feeling of being loved in a way that the mind has not yet categorized and labeled. And yet it is so undeniably a feeling of love that one is suddenly overwhelmed by a sense that there is no suffering, no matter how real, or corporeal, or emotionally devastating, there is no suffering that can escape this love; there is no suffering too great that cannot be comforted by this love. And in that darkness, one comes to realize that one has gotten the understanding of God all backward. God no longer exists to eradicate human pain and suffering. But in that very real, human pain and suffering, God's infinite love is there to hold us, embrace us and comfort us no matter how severe the pain is. One suddenly realizes the significance of Jesus' crucifixion, not so much from the standpoint of theoretical "substitutional atonement," but from the perspective of infinite love holding and sustaining finite humanity, even in the moment of death. And the brilliant light of that moment exposes all else in one's world as darkness. It is thoroughly confusing to realize that there is no other way to this point than through suffering, and an understanding that one has no power or control over any aspect of that journey to and through the pain.

What makes this such a dark and devastating place is that one recognizes that one has begun this journey precisely because of one's love for and by God. It all began in a love relationship. Somewhere back in Sunday School, we all learned that "God is love" (1Jn 4:8). But that is not the whole of it. Perhaps we might all agree that to express something, anything about the ineffable, we could use words like love to express what we "know" of God by virtue of what we have experienced of God. But that hardly comes close to the real thing. God and God's infinite capacity for love is the source of an unending and unstoppable outpouring of love. God, in love, or more correctly, as love, created life and all within it. However the distinction must be drawn between the *infinite* love, which is God and the *finite* love we feel and identify as creatures of God. The imbalance that these two elements of love creates, seeks to balance itself through a continual flow of love from the infinite to the finite.[68] And as James Finley says, "The infinite love which is the architect of our soul will be satisfied with nothing less than infinite love."[69]

John of the Cross explains that we have to be stripped of our addiction to the finite (our preconceived notions and expectations) many times. Mostly, John explains, this occurs through the loss of our senses, in what he calls the "purification of the appetites." For John of the Cross, the appetites are the five senses fueled by the desire for gratification. In other words it is not the desire for taste or the pleasure that tasting brings, but the desire to be gratified by tasting; not the desire for hearing birds singing nor the pleasure of hearing birds sing but the desire to be gratified by birds singing.[70] Ultimately what this means for the person on this inward quest of loving is that one must be purified from the desire to be satisfied and gratified by the love one receives from God. It is not the desire to love God or to be loved by God of which one must be purified, but rather the desire to be gratified by it, as if *we* somehow know what is best for our souls. We have had warming moments with God, moments of inner enlightenment and moments of intimacy with God. But what John of the Cross is saying is that we seekers of oneness must somehow be stripped of the notion that whatever we think the love of God might be, is what will be satisfying or gratifying in the end. Once again the ego/self has confined God by a finite concept of what would be gratifying. If only I could get this sign from God; we think, if only God would do such and so, then I would be gratified. It is not a grandiose idea (I don't ask for much) but it is a human/mortal and finite idea placed as a structure on the infinite. This is what John of the Cross says we must have stripped away in the purification of the appetites; our need to say what is, what must be; what conditions satisfy, as if we know. "We must remember at all costs that desire is not destroyed... desire is being purified, transformed, and carried into deeper, more integrated passion."[71]

As a result of this purification one finds oneself on a quest of love to seek union with the ultimate source of love; armed with clues resulting from one's past glimpses and experiences of love, and finding out that none of that matters,

---

[68] Recall, for example, the biology experiments we all did in high school where a leaf was placed in pure water. The imbalance of pure water on the outside of a leaf cell and substance-filled water inside the cell resulted in a flow of pure water into the cell, swelling it to capacity.

[69] Finley, CAC lecture.

[70] Finley, CAC lecture.

[71] FitzGerald, *Impasse*, 102.

that in fact all of that is *made up*, irrelevant and in the way.[72] What is experienced in this loss, what is experienced in in letting go of the need for gratification and any hope of getting it right, is a deep sense of loss and a feeling of being utterly unable to control the least bit of one's life. One is left powerless and seemingly helpless. And this is what is most terrifying in the dark night of the soul! Each time the individual becomes attached to or enraptured with a new experience, a new and fresher vision of the Divine, one's tendency is to attach too much significance to it and confuse that experience with the reality that is God.

However that is no indictment or rationale to give up the quest. It simply is the first indication that it is the *process* not the *end* that is important, despite the fact that it is the end point of union in relationship with God which is the focus of the entire journey to begin with. But what becomes clear is that the dark night of the soul appears to be neither a period of dysfunction in the spirituality of the believer, nor is it a period where God plays some twisted spiritual version of hide-and-seek. Rather what comes into the light at this point is that the dark night of the soul is a key dynamic in the process of the spiritual journey toward union with the incomprehensible all. "The transformational dynamic, the engine of human development," writes Loder, "is at best a reflection of the Holy Spirit."[73] The ultimate net effect of the dark night of the soul is a transformation of the little self into the big SELF in God.

Studies in the field of psychology show that transformation (previously in this thesis defined as deep moral/ethical/spiritual disruption) is always a process of sloughing off the previously functional belief system in order to take on a new and more complex level of understanding. In a sense, it is a death-rebirth process. That sloughing off of previously held ideals, beliefs and constructs produces a perception of extreme mental and emotional anguish, which some say feels like dying (as FitzGerald describes in her work on *Impasse*),[74] but which is a necessary ordeal in order for the individual to move to a deeper understanding. In other words, the spaces in between, the liminal space, where faith is questioned and the relationship with God feels jeopardized, may actually be natural consequences – or more accurately, the *cause* – of one's movement in spiritual development. Each trip through the dark night is a transformative experience and ultimately leads to a full transformation of the individual's being

---

[72] In the final (6th) chapter of this thesis we will see how even creeds and orthodox theology appears to the seeker as fiction that gets in the way of the experience of connection with the Divine.

[73] Loder, *Logic of the Spirit*, 244.

[74] FitzGerald, *Impasse*, 106.

– from identifying with "self" to becoming "SELF." Thus recurrences of the dark night of the soul are described differently and carry differing intensities on each successive pass through, depending on the transformational work being done at that point in the believer's life and the personal/cognitive style with which one processes them.[75]

However this is not the end of the dark night. Having lost words as the tools of meaning making only marks the beginning of the entry into the dark night. The darkness that follows, says John of the Cross, is like the deep darkness that is exposed via bright light. While our minds are suddenly illuminated by the "aha" of letting go, what we now see is that our understanding *is* the darkness and that our trials are not even close to being over. "Just so it is with the soul in this condition when it sees itself moved by the abundance of spiritual blessings yet and being unable to see the root of the imperfection and impurity which still remain within it, thinks it's trials are over."[76]

While it may be that contemplation of the love of God may bring on the dark night, these practices now have failed the seeker. John of the Cross offers little in the way of consolation, but rather asserts that this sign (not being able to meditate any longer) along with the lack of focus and a sincere desire to be alone, are together the three signs that one must now turn to the contemplation of the Spirit.[77] But this new style of contemplation is one of mindlessness and unknowing. "The less they understand however, the farther they penetrate into the night of the Spirit, whereof we are treating in this book, through which they must pass in order to be united with God, in a union that transcends all knowledge."[78] Contemplation at this point is learning to be still in God even when it feels like one is doing nothing at all. It is important to persist in this contemplative state irrespective of any sense of "productivity," says John of the Cross, because this is the state in which one is becoming receptive to what God is doing through love inside the soul.

---

[75] Westerhoff makes the point in his text, *Spiritual Life*, that approaches to spirituality vary depending on the personality of the individual. Using the Myers-Briggs Type Indicator as a model, he distinguishes mostly between thinking and feeling types, but the case can be made even more emphatically for intuitive and sensate types. Intuitive types tend to look for the similarities between constructs (this is like that) and may approach their personal theology from a more apophatic thought system (comfortable with the unknown and vague) while more sensate types construct their logic by looking at the differences between concepts (this is not that) and thus may be more cataphatic in their theological approach, seeking hard facts. Pages 59-62.

[76] John of the Cross, *Dark Night of the Soul*, Translation by Allison Peers (Mineola, NY: Dover Publications, 1953/2003), 56.

[77] John of the Cross, *Ascent*, 116.

[78] John of the Cross, *Ascent*, 120.

As seekers we still feel a need to do something to become worthy of the transformation that God is performing in us, but John of the Cross clearly cautions us to let go. Even though his instructions are to deny oneself of the desires, he instructs that doing so is not for the purpose of gaining favor or status with God. "The soul has a great desire to be a martyr and to show his love for God as a martyr does."[79] He goes on to say, "since these manifestations of knowledge come to the soul suddenly, and independently of its own free will, it must neither desire to have them nor desire not to have them, but must merely be humble and resigned concerning them, and God will perform his works how and when he wills… for the means must be humility and suffering for love of God with resignation as regards all reward."[80]

At some point in the contemplative process, one is bound to feel that God is communicating some message of import. But again John of the Cross cautions the seeker not to hastily interpret this as a sign. More often than not it is the mind attempting to find some significance in the nothingness that appears to be happening. "Some souls with the very smallest experience of meditation may say, 'God sent this to me,' or 'God answered me,' whereas it is not so it all, but as we have said, it is for the most part that they are saying into themselves."[81] The key in distinguishing whether something is actually coming as an insight from God is the nature of the feeling that accompanies the insight. Most certainly the "aha" is not a supernatural insight. But "if the soul desires to employ its faculties actively on the supernatural apprehensions (John of the Cross's word for insights gained through this process), it would do nothing less than abandon what it had already done, in order to do it again, neither would it enjoy what it had done nor could it produce any other result, by these actions of its own, save that of frustrating what has been done already."[82] A few pages later he explains that the body can only recall bodily images not spiritual images. "Now after the soul has had an experience of one of these apprehensions it can't recall it whatsoever it will, and this is not by the effigy and image that the apprehension has left in bodily sense, for, since this is of bodily form, as we say, it has no capacity for spiritual forms."[83]

This annihilation of meaning making, of language and of images is a process over time. One by one our foundations are taken away through repeated

---

[79] John of the Cross, *Ascent*, 157.

[80] John of the Cross, *Ascent*, 197.

[81] John of the Cross, *Ascent*, 210.

[82] John of the Cross, *Ascent*, 252.

[83] John of the Cross, *Ascent*, 255.

trips into the dark night. John of the Cross says that until and unless one is totally stripped of the "appetites," the desire to seek satisfaction through the will, or to make logical sense of these insights and experiences, one must fear that one will still be internally motivated to claim credit for the insight that is given in the dark night. "The Christian must then realize that the value of his good works, fasts, all names, penances, etc., is not based on the number or the quality of them, but upon the love of God which inspires him to do them. Wherefore the heart must not be sent upon pleasure, consolation and delight, and the other interests which good works and practices commonly bring with them, but it must concentrate on its rejoicing upon God."[84]

By turning one's focus continually toward loving God in the way God loves us (that is continually, totally, and unconditionally), the seeker of divine union in love will be able to attain the three virtues of this life: faith, hope and love. The destruction of understanding and meaning-making results in faith. Faith then becomes the operative dynamic that begins illuminating the mind by exposing historical experiences and ultimately exposing the folly of will. The purging of memory (remembered experiences, or the "Cloud of Forgetting" as *The Cloud* calls it) results in hope. The annihilation of will results in love. No longer is evidence needed to have faith, no longer is experience required to have hope and, no longer is the self the source and center of love. Through the dark night of the senses, the beginner starts letting go of the need for satisfaction from "getting it right." And through the dark night of the spirit, the soul is purged of self-will and self-referential meaning making. This process happens over time and through repeated, transformative trips into and out of the dark night. But so strong are our will and our ego, it seems, that it is hardly ever a linear process.

Summary of the Dark Night

John of the Cross's contention is that we are drawn forth into the night by God whose intent is to strengthen and confirm the virtues of the soul and convert it to the full service of God.[85] This pull, says Gerald May, is because the in-dwelling God, which has been with us since our beginnings, is becoming manifest in us as adults. But because of our developmental process of individuation, we have grown distant and separate from that truth and love; "we are asleep to the truth [and have] misplace[d] our love."[86]

---

[84] John of the Cross, *Ascent*, 293.

[85] John of the Cross, *Dark Night of the Soul*, translated by E. Allison Peers, Dover Thrift Editions, Paul Negri, General Editor, T.N.R. Rogers, Editor of the Volume (Mineola, NY: Dover Publications, 2003), 4.

[86] May, *Dark Night*, 51.

John of the Cross drew on the motif of night to describe this process, despite the fact that the "night" may go on for a protracted length of time, even years. He says that it is called the night for two reasons: that the nature of God is obscured and always has been (note the many times in the Bible where God is shrouded in a dense cloud and darkness) and because the light of God's divine presence exposes our sin and darkness.[87] Moreover, night is that time when our dreams and nightmares arise. It is a time, since childhood, when we feel most alone. But most of all night represents the darkness – or the absence of light. This, according to John of the Cross, is not because there is no light. In fact, like Lao Tzu's bright light, it casts the darkest shadow.[88] John of the Cross writes, "the brighter and purer is supernatural and Divine light, the more it darkens the soul."[89] In other words, our darkness is only dark in contrast to the light of the Divine. The ego becomes conscious through this process of having separated itself from the rest of humanity and from God. "The darkness and other evils of which the soul is conscious when Divine light strikes it are not darkness and evils caused by this light, but pertain to the soul itself and the light illuminates it so that it may see them."[90]

With this powerful infusion of good and light, the soul experiences great pain, which John of the Cross describes in two ways. The first he equates to the pain of having a bright light shone in your eyes when you have been in the darkness. In the presence of this pure and intense goodness and light, the soul shrieks in pain. The second pain John of the Cross names is the pain of weakness. When we are confronted by the power of God, which "assails the soul with such a certain force… it suffers such pain in its weakness that it nearly swoons away."[91] It is not that God delights in our human suffering and pain or even desires that we experience pain, but it is true "that wounded and rejected people have a much greater chance of seeing clearly. Beyond the illusions of their ego-constructed world views," writes Richard Rohr, "wisdom emerges from what you do with your pain!"[92] Additionally, Rohr contends, "The private ego will resist and rationalize in every way that it can. My experience is that, apart from suffering,

---

[87] John of the Cross, *Dark Night*, 47.

[88] An often quoted adage from the Tao Te Ching is "the brightest light casts the darkest shadows."

[89] John of the Cross, *Dark Night*, 58.

[90] John of the Cross, *Dark Night*, 77.

[91] John of the Cross, *Dark Night*, 49.

[92] Rohr, *Things Hidden*, 101.

failure, humiliation, and pain, none of us will naturally let go of our self-sufficiency. We will think that our story is just about *us*. It isn't."[93]

The Bible provides, in the book of Job, a mythical account of one man's experience of a protracted journey through the dark night experience. Job lays out a unique and different question in the face of human development. Specifically, Job (the book) poses the hypothetical question; will humans be religious (believe in God or maintain spirituality) in the total absence of any contact - reward or punishment from God? It is an investigation into the experience of the dark night, not by one whose course was set on religious vocation, but by what we might see as a regular man. To make certain that there is no dualistic interpretation of right and wrong, the author of Job describes him as a blameless and upright man who feared God and shunned evil. Job did nothing to warrant his dark night – he neither sought it (he only wanted to worship and praise God) nor deserved it (Job 1:1).[94]

As the story opens, Job has lost everything to which he is attached – his family, children, cattle, sheep and all his possessions. His wife and friends turn against him and he is left with absolutely nothing. Job's despair and grief are so profound that he tears his robes and asks God to kill him – he cannot stand the pain of his loss. But these are not the source of his dark night. What ensues in the story of Job is that as he prays at first for vindication – his day in court if you will – so that he might understand the reason he suffers. Ultimately he asks God for the relief of death to end his suffering, God does not answer. There are no sounds, no signs that God even hears his cries. This John of the Cross says is the first sign of the dark night experience – the dryness and impotence of one's spiritual life.[95] Like Job, John of the Cross identifies this as a spiritual pain closely associated with the pain and grief of loss. The joy of having once had a fulfilling and nurturing relationship with God is gone. We find that prayer dries up not because God is not listening but because it is not a prayer from our being – it is more a performing of prayer, a "doing" of prayer rooted in our words and ideas which must give way and cease to exist in order to get to a new way of being in intimate relationship with God.

In this pain, John of the Cross says, we are visited by several spirits. The first is a spirit of fornication (not so much in a sexual connotation but rather any self-indulgent pursuit, as May translates it,[96] or of gluttony as described by John

---

[93] Rohr, *Job*, 158

[94] All Biblical references are taken from *The New Oxford Annotated Bible, Revised Standard Version*, (Oxford: Oxford University Press), 2001.

[95] May, *Dark Night*, 92.

[96] May, *Dark Night*, 143.

of the Cross). John contends that this is because we have grown to enjoy the pleasure which human nature takes in spiritual things.[97]

Faced with the dryness and emptiness that marks the dark night's beginning, the seeker is tempted to find *anything* pleasurable, or at least not painful. Thomas Merton has a slightly different take on this spirit. He says that the spiritual high one gets when we get even a glimpse of true spiritual connection is a seduction that we tend to hang on to. "This taste for 'experiences' can be one of the most dangerous obstacles in [one's] interior life. It is the rock on which many who might have become contemplatives have ended in shipwreck."[98] When the spirit of gluttony or fornication proves to be empty, it is followed by another John of the Cross calls the spirit of blasphemy. This is seen at its fullest in the rest of the Job story. The reader can almost hear Job screaming in the text, "I loathe my life... I will speak in bitterness of my soul... (10:1)" [and turning his rage directly at God] "*Let me alone*, that I may find a little comfort before I go, never to return, to the land of gloom and deep darkness, the land of gloom and chaos where light is like darkness (10:20-22)." In the pit of despair, John of the Cross knew well what any human would do – we would curse our maker. But he makes it clear that "it is not God who disappears, but only our concepts, images and sensations of God."[99] Job, in his final despair says, "My soul is poured out within me; days of affliction have taken hold of me. The night racks my bones, and the pain that gnaws me takes no rest. With violence he seizes my garment; he grasps me by the collar of my tunic; he has cast me into the mire, and I have become like dust and ashes (30:16-19)."

This marks the onset of the final spirit John of the Cross describes. The *"spirit vertiginis"* comes as the seeker becomes the sought – as the dark night moves from any pretense of active to the totally passive aspect of being acted upon. Merton says that we *have* to let go of trying. "When it comes to fighting the deep and unconscious habits of attachment which we can hardly dig up and recognize, all our meditations, self examinations, resolutions and planned campaigns may not only be ineffective but may sometimes lend assistance to our enemies, because it may easily happen that our resolutions may be dictated by the vice we need to get rid of."[100] Suddenly the tables are turned; the seeker is fully emptied and realizes nothing can be done of his or her own accord. The soul itself can no longer meditate on or understand what is happening and why. The

---

[97] John of the Cross, *Dark Night*, 11.

[98] Merton, *New Seeds*, 247.

[99] May, *Dark Night*, 146.

[100] Merton, *New Seeds*, 257.

individual – the ego – surrenders; gives up, and God begins to communicate directly with the soul, bypassing any conscious awareness. This totally upside-down and backward experience is so dizzying and disorienting that spiritual teacher and author, Carolyn Myss calls it "spiritual madness."[101] John of the Cross says that it "fills the person with a thousand scruples and perplexities, so confounding that they can never be satisfied."[102] It is a feeling of being in total darkness, like the early experiments of Gestalt psychology where people were placed in a room of total darkness. Without any referent of direction, individuals became physically nauseous. When presented with a single (fixed) point of light in a room of total darkness, they reported it moving around so much that it made them dizzy. Likewise, in the darkness of this night, where God is directly at work rearranging our innards, the dizziness becomes overwhelming – not only can we not see, we know something is happening and cannot identify location, source or subject. It is always darkest just before the dawn, as the adage goes.

In the complexity of post-modern life, spiritual seekers may not see or experience the dark night of the soul in exactly the way John of the Cross has so neatly laid it out. It may, however, in fact be a process that is more attached to our common humanity than to our spiritual journeys. The dark night of the soul, as a transformative psychological experience may be catalyzed by any social or interpersonal experience, impasse or loss – not solely by contemplation as *The Cloud* and John of the Cross contend. FitzGerald writes that, "in every significant relationship, we come to the experience of limitation, our own and others'. We come to the point where we must withdraw and reclaim our projections of God, of friend, of ministry, of community, and let the 'others' be who and what they are: mystery."[103]

Thus, despite the brilliant detail of John of the Cross' description of the dark night of the soul, there seems to be no predictability from one event to another nor seemingly is there any similarity from one individual's experience to another's. Jacob's dark night was a single night, Job's went on for years, as did Joseph's. My own personal dark nights came and went many times over the course of my adult life. Temporally, there are no similarities. But a broader view of the dark night process, woven from strands of John of the Cross, *The Cloud of Unknowing*, and the modern mystics cited herein, shows a definitive process of stripping away successive layers of "knowing" and of egoic willfulness in a way that opens the soul/SELF up to the influx of the love of God. The clear result from the dark night of the soul is a transformed spirituality. One no longer sees God as

---

[101] Carolyn Myss, *Spiritual Madness*, Sounds True Recordings, 2002.

[102] May, *Dark Night*, 149.

[103] FitzGerald, *Impasse*, 101.

one once did; one no longer talks either about God or about oneself and one's spirituality they way one once did; and one no longer can relate to the world of other creatures of this God of transformation they way one once did. As a result of the dark night, everything changes.

While taking a much broader interpretation of the dark night of the soul may be enlightening, care must be taken not to expand the range too much. This thesis will stay fairly confined to the realm of the spiritual journey described at the outset, expanding only slightly on the classical definitions of John of the Cross and the nature of the onset of the dark nights. John of the Cross was a biblical scholar and relied on both the Old and New Testaments as sources for inspiration as well as guidance through his dark nights. In the following chapter, we will explore some of those texts to which he referred, seeking evidence of the dark night of the soul in the lives and stories of the Bible.

Chapter Two – No Longer Called Jacob
Insights from Scripture

So he said to him, "What is your name?" And he said, "Jacob." Then the man said, "You shall no longer be called Jacob, but Israel, for you have striven with God and with humans, and have prevailed."

Genesis 32:27-28 (New Oxford Annotated Bible)

Having experienced the dark night of the soul and its effects on one's faith in particular and one's worldview in general, the faithful seeker will look anew at both scripture and theology. The Bible, which previously has been a source of rules and commandments, becomes a tool for advancing insight and wisdom. Formerly contradictory passages become methods for holding the tension of non-dual (both/and) logic. But the question arises of whether there is guidance about this faith journey resulting from the dark night of the soul. Are there examples and biblical stories of persons enduring the dark night, and if so, what are the effects of having endured the dark night? What light do sacred texts shed on the effects of the dark night of the soul? Looking for examples of either the dark nights or the effects of the dark night may require some creative interpretation as one would be hard-pressed to find many exegetes who are conversant in the language of the dark night of the soul.

That notwithstanding, it would appear that the writers of the books of the bible were no strangers to the effects of the dark night. John of the Cross wrote that "So many passages of Scripture are there which could be cited to this purpose, that time and strength would fail us to write all of them, for all that can be said thereof is certainly less than the truth."[104] Though it is never named as such, the evidence of transformation of the biblical characters' way of being is undeniable. These early writers did not have the language of human psychology from which to describe their characters' transformation. Often stories tell a before-and-after type of tale where, after some trial/ordeal which we might imagine is a dark night experience, the protagonist acts and speaks in entirely differently and out of character ways after whatever may (or must) have happened in the intervening time. The myth of Job is a classic example of this. (Though Job's story was outlined previously in this paper, it warrants briefly repeating here for illustrative purposes). For most of the story, Job is seen as a man seeking justice. He has, not only by his own accounting, but by the accounts of his friends and even the narrator of the story, lived a most righteous and generous life. What could he have done to warrant such a fate – the death of his family, the loss of his flocks, his home and his status? So for the better part of thirty chapters, Job demands his day in court. His rants, which started out as angry demands, end with a surrendering death wish. Ultimately, Job falls silent and we can only assume

---

[104] John of the Cross, *Dark Night*, 53.

falls into the darkest night of his long ordeal. Because when next we hear from him, Job is a totally different man. He is humble and not in the least bit self-righteous. He admits his lack of understanding, to having tried to make mortal sense of divine logic. He finally sees that what he "knows" is so little in comparison to what there is to be known. Job has been transformed.

It would appear (in my opinion) that, lacking the vocabulary of transformation and psychology, biblical writers used three forms to denote the transformation of their characters. The first is that there is a period wherein the character is absent from the narrative story (usually another person is introduced or another story told) as is the case with Job or as we shall see with Elijah. A second technique is that the character is given or adopts a new name representative of this new way of being as one sees with Jacob/Israel and Saul/Paul. Thirdly, being transformed can be represented as the characters being totally unrecognizable by even their most intimate friends or family, as one sees in the story of Joseph or the risen Jesus.[105]

The book of Genesis lays out a series of stories that all seem to carry some element of the dark night transformation. The namesake for this paper is a story of one dark night of the soul experienced by Jacob. In the story, Jacob, who had tricked and stolen his way to fortune and family, had been running from his father-in-law from whom he and his wives had stolen flocks and household goods. Jacob, who feared reproach from his father-in-law on one side and the wrath of his brother Esau (whose rightful inheritance he had also deceitfully stolen) on the other side, had sent his family and flocks off ahead to Canaan for safety. That night Jacob experienced his famous wrestling match. We don't know much about the writer of this story but the message is dark and multilayered. God chooses as the father of the twelve tribes the most unlikely of heroes – a liar, cheater, philanderer and swindler – and renames him Israel. In the dark night, Jacob is called to account for his deeds as he struggles for his life. The net result, his dislocated hip (say some interpretations) or his wounded manhood (according to others) left him incapable of the hit-and-run life he had led up to that point and placed him on a path of leadership.

But neither Jacob's story nor the myth of Job are the only dark night stories in the Bible. Many of the most powerful events happen in a fearful night – from the Passover of the Angel of Death to the birth of Jesus.[106] Even the

---

[105] In the final chapter, A Theology of the Dark Night" I will contend that Jesus' commandment to "follow me" is an invitation into a death/resurrection experience so profound that he could only make that point through actual physical death. Thus I look at the journey of Jesus' ministry as a dark night journey.

[106] I would contend that being displaced and homeless with an expectant and unwed young woman in a time of rigid and violent moral codes may have been more than a bit frightening for Joseph and his betrothed teenaged companion!

crucifixion though occurring at midday, became "as dark as night." Theologian, Barbara Brown Taylor writes, "Once you start noticing how many important things happen at night in the Bible, the list grows fast... This [Biblical] view of darkness is far more nuanced than the one that demonizes darkness. While this darkness is dangerous, it is as sure a sign of God's presence as brightness is, which makes the fear of it different from the fear of snakes and robbers."[107] And, lest we forget, even the creation story begins with darkness before the creator spoke light into it. Biblical darkness and dark nights seem to have less of a sinister nature to them and more of a holiness or sacredness. But let's take a brief look at some of the other stories and events that might be considered "dark nights of the soul" for the characters of the Bible and in particular to the before and after picture we have of the lead character.

In the following interpretations of classical Biblical stories, I will be drawing on my own reflections as much as on established Biblical commentaries. My method was to approach the Bible from the perspective that it may have been written as a tool for teasing out reactions and for inspiring (even pushing) spiritual development as opposed to a document of literal accounts and rules for living. Starting with that assumption and using *Lectio Divina* as my spiritual practice for reflection on the scriptures, I began looking more creatively and interpretively at the texts.

Abraham and Isaac

One of the earliest encounters of the type of spiritual tests we find in the dark night of the soul is when Abraham,[108] finally blessed with a son from his elderly wife, hears God ask him to do the unthinkable act of sacrificing Isaac. While neither in the night nor an experience of the absence of the Divine, this story certainly calls our logic to task. How, after making the covenant to have Abraham's offspring more numerous than the nighttime stars, would this God require the slaughter of Abraham's only son through whom such a covenant would most likely occur? I always found it curious that classical art portrayed Abraham, with the knife held in the air, as either angry-looking or reverently looking upward toward the heavens. Were I in such a situation, I can only imagine that with tears of anguish streaming down my face, I would be aiming the knife at my own chest rather than taking the life of my beloved son. Though we can

---

[107] Taylor, *Learning to Walk*, 45,47.

[108] The author gives readers a clue that this is the story of a transformed man by having God rename Abram as Abraham. Perhaps (as was the case with Jacob/Israel) this is the most effective way for the ancients to indicate transformation, though, as it will be shown, transformation is also indicated as having visibly changed into an unrecognizable personage (as we will see with Joseph and the resurrected Jesus).

conjecture the zeitgeist to be different several millennia ago, or that theophany carried a greater weight or reality to the ancients, it still pitted an elderly man whose life was nearly over against the love of his life and his only son by order of a test of faith. It had to be the transformative moment for Abraham however it played out. It would have been the darkest hour of his soul.

All in the family – the story of Joseph

Joseph was the son of Jacob (thus the great-grandson of Abraham) and one of the few characters the Bible describes as remarkably handsome. Joseph's trouble all begins with his night visions. Though his brothers already disliked him because of his favored status with their father, he became despised once he started talking about his dreams. In one such dream Joseph's teenaged ego has his brothers' sheaves of wheat all bowing to his wheat, and his retelling of the dream-story literally infuriates them. His brothers at first plotted to kill him, but instead sold him into slavery to a passing caravan. Nothing is said of Joseph until he resurfaces as the purchase of the captain of the royal guard. Because "the Lord was with him" Joseph was rapidly promoted and ultimately given charge over the captain's entire household. However, because of his good looks, the captain's wife rather fancied him and tried several times to seduce him. When spurned in her attempts the last time, she accused Joseph of attempted rape.

This landed Joseph in the royal prison for several years where we are told only that he was somewhat first among the prisoners because the lord was with him.[109] Joseph interprets the dreams of two of his cellmates but is not remembered for his talent until a few years later when Pharaoh himself has a baffling dream. Joseph is called for, washed up, shaved and given some clothes (further indicators of the ordeal he had endured). Not only does Joseph give an answer to the confusing dream, but offers a plan for dealing with the coming famine. But there is something about his character that has Pharaoh see God in Joseph. Again, because of his skills, Joseph is advanced and ultimately given the daughter of the high priestess as a wife.

We are told that Joseph has forgotten the pain of his imprisonment and hardships, but when his brothers come seeking food during the famine, Joseph is tempted to get some revenge. Nonetheless, his compassion is quickly evident as he weeps for his family. Furthermore, he is so transformed by his ordeals that his own brothers do not recognize him (though he immediately recognizes them, presumably because they have not changed much over the years). When he can

---

[109] One might conjecture that even in a place of being favored among the prisoners, Joseph was *in fact* a prisoner and not in some luxurious spa! It had to have been a place of despair, even for one as devoted to God as Joseph might have been.

stand the charade no longer he reveals himself to his amazed and shocked brothers hugging, kissing and crying in their embraces.

What could possibly have produced this kind of compassion except for the deep-rooted spiritual transformation of the dark night of the soul? Though we are told that the Lord never left him, what we know from research (and shall see in later chapters) is that it is the perception of the ego in the dark night that makes it appear or feel as though God has abandoned them. One feels distant from God's love and care because of the anguish of the moment. Joseph's transformation gave him the ability to intermarry with another religious sect and see the presence of God's work even in the Pharaoh. Only one who had been moved to a universalized level of operating could have done that.

Elijah

Moving on from Genesis, we again see the classic pattern of the dark night of the soul in Elijah's story. Prophets of old were not clairvoyants who foretold the future, but rather were individuals who spoke to the masses for God. By definition then Elijah would have gotten regular theophonic transmissions for delivery to his people. It was not so much that the prophet felt a close, beloved relationship with God but that he had a regular interaction with his "employer." As the spokesperson for the God of Israel, Elijah had been in the habit of warning the Israelites of the southern kingdom of God's wrath against them for their polytheism. It was commonplace for people of the time to worship Yahweh as the God of Gods but in as much as Yahweh had no specific jurisdiction over such earthly things as fertility and nature, they turned to Baal whom they believed did hold that power. Elijah's main call was to turn the people back to the worship of Yahweh as the one supreme God.

The storied Yahweh versus Baal smackdown at Mount Carmel was Elijah's demonstration that, in fact, Yahweh did reign supreme over all other Gods. As a result of a rather decidedly unanimous decision in the contest, Elijah had revengefully decreed that the prophets of Baal be put to death. When word of the slaughter of Baal's prophets reached Jezebel, she retaliated by ordering the death of Elijah, who ran in fear for his life.

Thus began Elijah's dark night experience. He wandered into the desert and prayed for his death (one is left to speculate what pain or distress he might have been feeling to lead to such a request). But he fell asleep and was awakened by an angel to urged him to eat in preparation for his ordeal to come (twice, as reported in 1 Kings 19:5-8). After he woke up the third time Elijah set off one a long[110] and arduous trek through the desert to Mount Horeb (Mount Sinai, the mountain of God, where Moses received the ten commandments). There, Elijah found the cave that Moses used and waited for God to come back to him.

It is significant to note that Elijah had no dialog with God from the time of the duel with Baal until he finally heard the question (in a style similar to the question put to Adam), "What are you doing here?" in the cave on Mount Horeb. Elijah twice insisted that he was a condemned man and was hiding to save his life. In a strange third person theophany Elijah is told to go out of the cave and wait for the lord to pass by (another direct tie to the Moses tradition of God allowing one of God's elite to see the lord only as a passing event). But unlike all of Elijah's previous encounters with God, Yahweh does not come as a terrifyingly powerful event (fire, wind or earthquakes). Instead the prophet hears the "sound of sheer silence"[111] which Elijah immediately recognizes as God's presence. As a result of this encounter, we might assume that Elijah had "seen the light" of transformation but when asked a third time why he is here, Elijah sticks to his story of being hunted down. In the end, God sends Elijah off to anoint his successor.

However, the mythology and legend that surrounds Elijah especially in the Jewish tradition portrays the prophet as a transformed messenger. His message of patience and compassion lives on in the tradition of setting an extra chair for Elijah at all covenant ceremonies (Seders, circumcisions, etc.). Rabbis will often hold off on a difficult decision to wait for Elijah to weigh in (often meaning that the rash, first judgment will not happen and a more compassionate one would be rendered instead). Thus, while the actual scriptural references to Elijah in 1 Kings 17-19 and the beginning few chapters of 2 Kings seems somewhat unchanged (where he is still portrayed as the angry prophet of doom and gloom), the net effect of the prophet's transformed and more compassionate message lives on in midrashic tradition.

David and The Psalmists

Studying the life of David, from the many attempts on his life to his pain and grief experienced at the death of his best friend Jonathan and later the deaths of his sons, one might infer that the great monarch must have had his fair share of dark night periods. But the texts that actually chronicle his life do not provide

---

[110] The biblical number 40 is used to represent a long time, as in it rained for 40 days and nights, the Jews wandered for 40 years in the desert, and Jesus fasted for 40 days. Elijah's ordeal of hiking (without food) for 40 days is a similar reference to "a long time."

[111] The New Oxford Annotated Bible uses this phrase instead of the "faint whisper" or "a gentle blowing" cited in other translations.

sufficient information to actually support that hypothesis. And though many of the first Psalms (up through Psalm 72) include the inscription "of David," the debate is still open as to whether he was actually the author of those. Nonetheless, if one were to consider the Psalms in part to be either written by David or about the life of the great king, one sees within their verses a wonderful expression of the absence/presence cycle reflective of the dark night of the soul. Analyses of the Psalms often break them into Psalms of lament, Psalms of ascent, and wisdom Psalms, and it is the former that provide a language of the suffering felt when one feels estranged from the love of God.

The Psalms of lament, whether individual or communal address the feeling of desolation when faced with life's perils in the absence of God (e.g., Ps. 22, "My God, my God, why have you forsaken me?"). Throughout the Psalms, God's presence is presented more often as the cavalry coming to the rescue (Ps 17:13 "Rise up, O Lord, confront them, overthrow them! By your sword deliver my life from the wicked.") than as the presence of healing love (Ps 26:3 "for your steadfast love is before my eyes." and Ps 36:7 "How precious is your steadfast love, O God."). But when the Psalmist feels the absence of God's powerful presence, he[112] turns to despair and depression as seen in the opening lines of Psalm 22 or of this lament:

Psalm 69
[1] Save me, O God,
    for the waters have come up to my neck.
[2] I sink in deep mire,
    where there is no foothold;
I have come into deep waters
    and the flood sweeps over me.
[3] I am weary with my crying;
    my throat is parched.
My eyes grow dim
    with waiting for my God.

If the Psalms are thought of as reflections from a traveler through the dark night of the soul, then one should find evidence within them of the wisdom that results from such transformative experiences. However because of the editing processes in the construction of the Book of Psalms,[113] the wisdom Psalms do not follow in any particular order, e.g. directly after a deep and gut-wrenching lament,

---

[112] Again, assuming the authorship of David.
[113] Commentary in the New Oxford Annotated Bible suggests that the collection of psalms as an ordered text, divided into five segments like the Pentateuch, is more a device for facilitating their use in worship and not reflective of their chronology or actual intent.

or as a group of the later Psalms. Furthermore, being the collected work of several authors (as opposed to being the sole authorship of David) might also make the task of finding an outcome of one author's dark night more difficult. However, that notwithstanding, there seem to be several psalms that represent the kind of universalizing thought that often results form dark night experiences. Take for example Ps 37:8 "Refrain from anger and forsake wrath. Do not fret – it leads only to evil." A great example of post dark night wisdom is found in the first three stanzas of Psalm 49.

> Hear this, all you peoples;
>> give ear, all inhabitants of the world,
> both low and high,
>> rich and poor together.
> My mouth shall speak wisdom;
>> the meditation of my heart shall be understanding.
> I will incline my ear to a proverb;
>> I will solve my riddle to the music of the harp.
>
> Why should I fear in times of trouble,
>> when the iniquity of my persecutors surrounds me,
> those who trust in their wealth
>> and boast of the abundance of their riches?
> Truly, no ransom avails for one's life,
>> there is no price one can give to God for it.
> For the ransom of life is costly,
>> and can never suffice,
> that one should live on forever
>> and never see the grave.
>
> When we look at the wise, they die;
>> fool and dolt perish together
> and leave their wealth to others.
>> Their graves or their homes forever,
> their dwelling places to all generations,
>> though they named lands their own.
> Mortals cannot abide in their pomp;
>> they are like the animals that perish.

In this Psalm, one sees that the author clearly understands the unity of all things. Contrary to the prevailing belief of the time – that the rich are different and blessed by God – the psalmist sees equality of all persons and even of all creation (in the twice repeated verse "Mortals cannot abide in their pomp; they are like the animals that perish." – verses 12 and 20). The dark night has leveled the playing field with pain and suffering; and death is the great equalizer since, in the end, we all die.

> Oh Lord, God of my salvation,
> > when at night I cry out in your presence,
> let my prayer come before you;
> > incline your ear to my cry.
> For my soul is full of troubles,
> > and my life draws near to Sheol.
> For I am counted among those who go down to the pit;
> > I am like those who have no help,
> like those forsaken among the dead,
> > like those slain that lie in the grave,
> like those that you remember no more.
> > Psalm 88: 1-5

Other psalms like 127 express the futility of human effort ("Unless the Lord builds the house, those who build it labor in vain."), suggesting that God does the heavy work of development, or the unity of all as in the very short Song of Ascents," Psalm 133 ("How very good and pleasant it is when kindred live together in unity!"). Thus, while the Book of Psalms may have been ordered as liturgy, the contrast between the cries for vindication or of sorrow and despair in the laments on the one hand, and the trust and understanding that comes from a wisdom journey on the other hand, is evident throughout the text.

Isaiah, Jeremiah and The Lamentations

These three texts might be considered together as they represent their respective authors' attempt to deal with the events and emotions surrounding the conquest of Jerusalem and the exile of the Israelites. While I will not go into the actual historical events of the period (mid eighth century BCE through the end of the sixth century BCE), a full discussion of the dark night of a people's soul would be incomplete without a brief look at the impact of their exile.

Isaiah often wrote of the people's experience of the dark night in direct terms of light and darkness. For example, in 50:10 Isaiah wrote, "Who is among you that fears the Lord, that obeys the voice of his servant, that walks in darkness and hath no light?" And a bit later, "We wait for light, and lo! there is darkness; for brightness, but we walk in gloom. We grope for the wall like the blind along the wall, groping like those who have no eyes; we stumble at noon as in the twilight; among the vigorous as though we were dead." (Is 59:9-10). Isaiah

51

attributes such darkness to relying on legalistic dualism, saying "no one goes to the law honestly (Is 59:4)." It is always to prove some ego-driven point in self-righteousness. But when, in this darkness, the people find their way to God, they put down their warring ways and open their doors to others. "I will appoint Peace as your overseer and Righteousness as your taskmaster. Violence shall be heard no more in your land... The sun shall no longer be your light by day nor for brightness shall the moon give light to you by night, but the Lord will be your everlasting light, and your God will be your glory. (Is 60:18-19)"

Brueggemann calls Isaiah's style "poetic imagination" and claims that Isaiah is the supreme example of this powerful and transformative style of ministry. Too often Isaiah is misread as a prophet of the exile who is simply speaking of the overthrow of the Babylonians and the pain of the captive peoples of Israel. That is not what it is about at all, says Brueggemann. "The poetry is not aimed first of all at external conduct, as though the poet expected the people to immediately start packing for travel. Rather, the poetry cuts underneath behavior to begin to transform the self-image, communal image and the image of historical possibility."[114] By speaking from a place of transformation, the prophet is able to call others through the process of transformation as well.

> Two reference points are available for such a new way of speech. On the one hand, it is the text and the tradition which gives us the materials for metaphors. On the other hand, it is a present reality of pain which energizes and illuminates the metaphors. It is the interaction of remembered text and present pain that form the matrix out of which comes new speech. It is clear that 2 Isaiah's poetry is precisely such an interaction of text and pain.[115]

Isaiah speaks of God as one would after having gone through the dark night transformation. "Do not fear, for I have redeemed you; I have called you by name and you are mine. When you pass through the waters, I will be with you; and through the rives, they will not overwhelm you." (Is. 43:1-2) Isaiah knows that when he is put to the test, when he is up to his neck in alligators, when he is overwhelmed with grief, *that* is when he is closest to God. In the darkest hour God's lovingkindness and grace are most visible. God does not make the source of pain disappear, but rather God's passion and grace are there to support and uplift us in our times of trial.

---

[114] Walter Brueggemann, *Hopeful Imagination: Prophetic Voices in Exile* (Philadelphia: Fortress Press, 1986) 97.

[115] Brueggemann, *Hopeful Imagination*, 99.

Jeremiah functions in much the same way. As the author himself or as the often-assumed author of Lamentations, Jeremiah speaks from the depth of woundedness and pain. But he articulates the pain not as a statement of historical fact. Rather he states, and restates how painful this exile is, as if to bring it more into focus for the people. In order for the people to be moved into and through this transformation, the pain must be real. For Jeremiah, it appears as though the Israelites have become accustomed to being captive and have assimilated into the Babylonian culture. Jeremiah is issuing a wake-up call; a call to feel the pain and to know its horrible reality. But the reality of pain cannot and must not be smoothed over if we are intent on transformation. "Sweet talk, denial, and surface good news will not permit us to move across the pain that goes with such an ending. *Only grief permits newness*," says Brueggemann.[116]

The God of the Israelites had always been a rescuer; the Divine power that came swooping down to vanquish the foe and vindicate his chosen peoples. But to the student of the dark night, the perception of God as the puppeteer, as *deus ex machina*, is itself destroyed and a new understanding and relationship has taken its place. Brueggemann contends Jeremiah understood God as companion, not conqueror, and that it was his relationship with and immersion in the grief and pain of the present time that allowed him to see God in this different light. It is why Brueggemann refers to the exile prophets as purveyors of hope. They are not speaking of the hope for a rescue but rather of the genuine hope that is born in the depths of darkness when seemingly all hope is lost. "The future belongs to the desolate one who is surprised by the future" and hope is found by the hopeless one who is surprised by the presence of God in this desolate place.[117]

Jonah, the comic relief of the Dark Night

Though only four short chapters in length, any discussion of dark nights of the soul in the Old Testament would be incomplete without a mention of Jonah, the reluctant prophet. As a result of God's request to go and convert the Ninevites, Jonah takes off in flight in the opposite direction – toward Tarshish. Part of this trip involves a sea passage and it is on that leg of the trip that the ship on which Jonah was riding encountered an immense storm. Jonah immediately recognized this as his "punishment" and instructs the sailors to toss him into the sea. Being righteous and upstanding men, they flatly refuse and seek other options. But on the insistence of Jonah, they comply and heave him overboard.

---

[116] Brueggemann, *Hopeful Imagination*, 41.

[117] Brueggemann, *Hopeful Imagination*, 116.

There begins Jonah's dark night. No sooner is he overboard than God causes a large fish to swallow him, and in the belly of the fish, our hero sees the light! In a very psalm-like prayer, Jonah traces his descent into the pit and his subsequent free-fall into trust in the lord. "The waters closed in over me; the deep surrounded me... yet you brought up my life from the Pit, O Lord my God. As my life was ebbing away, I remembered the Lord." (Jonah, 2:5-7)

Something clearly happened in this moment of remembrance because as soon as Jonah is spit out of the fish and heads into the great city of Nineveh, he is able to convert nearly everyone with whom he speaks. So powerful is his speech that the King hears of it and orders everyone to repent – even the animals. (One can only imagine dogs and sheep wearing sackcloth and ashes at this point!) However that only infuriates Jonah who scolds God saying essentially, "I told you that is what would happen! That's why I ran away." Irrespective of the story line of conversion because of a transformed prophet, the irony of Jonah's displeasure at the will of God being fulfilled strikes the reader as counterintuitive. In fact did not Jonah run because he feared mockery? Clearly the writer is trying to make a point about the results of transformation. From the time of his release from the dark night of his fish belly, Jonah is completely different. And though his prophesy converts the immense city of Nineveh, his logic from that point on is counterintuitive and even ludicrous.

There are few commentaries on the book of Jonah through which one can look into the other meanings that might be inferred from the text. However one might posit that the author wishes to portray God as merciful and compassionate (to Nineveh) despite Jonah's disgust. Personally, I find the irony and twisted logic to be a delightful form of humor – poking fun at those who have gone through the dark night. Almost so that we do not canonize him, Jonah is made out to be a fool. Interestingly, St. Frances called himself "the Court Jester." And in many ways we who have passed through the dark night are fools. Surviving the dark night's death grip gives one a new and different view of the world. But one's tendency to speak in riddles about that which one has experienced and of concepts for which there are no effective words may indeed sound like backward logic and the type of nonsense we would accuse Jonah of having. We most likely do sound like gibberish and doubletalk!

Paul, the transformation of Saul of Tarsus

Turning to the New Testament, the most obvious dark night conversion story is that of Saul of Tarsus. It is a story that is so familiar that it almost does not need to be retold. Essentially, Saul, a devout Jew and Pharisee, had taken on the role of hunting down and arresting (even supervising the execution of) the followers of "the way," meaning the teachings of Jesus. While on one such hunting trip, along the road to Damascus, Saul was blinded by a brilliant light. Asking who was behind the light he heard the voice say it was Jesus the one he is persecuting. Saul is given instructions to go into Damascus to the house of Ananias and wait further instructions. For three days (again, one of those magically indicative biblical numbers like 40) Saul remained blinded and after Ananias prayed over him, and his sight was restored, Saul chose to change his name to his Roman name of Paul (we can only presume because of his interest in preaching in more Roman-dominated areas of the gentile world). Whatever the case, Paul became a new man and Saul as he had been known ceased to exist.

However, too often the Luke/Acts story of conversion on the road to Damascus is as far as readers push the story of Paul. But by his own accounting, Paul left Damascus and went on a walkabout in Arabia for an undisclosed amount of time before returning to Damascus where he stayed for another three years. But he neither talked with other Christians nor went to Jerusalem during that time (Gal. 1:16-19). He had to make sense of this radical disruption to his personal belief structure. Only then could he begin teaching and preaching his new theological perspective.

One need not exercise too much imagination to realize how terribly earthshattering this encounter was for Saul. He had been trained in Talmudic law[118] and was by his own description well "advanced in Judaism beyond many of my contemporaries… being more extremely zealous for my ancestral traditions." (Gal. 1:14) New Testament scholar, N.T. Wright contends that this very specific wording of Paul's indicates that he (Saul) was "acting out the model of Phinehas and/or Elijah. His zeal led him into physical violence against those whom he saw as the heirs and successors of the compromised Jews of Numbers 25 and the Baal worshipers of 1 Kings 18 (see Acts 22:3-5). He 'was persecuting the church with great violence and was trying to destroy it. (Gal. 1:13)'"[119] If Saul saw himself in the lineage of Elijah, Wright further contends, when stopped in his tracks on the way to Damascus, he would do as Elijah did: he would go back to the roots of his calling, to Mount Sinai (Horeb), which Paul cites later in Galatians 4:25, as being in Arabia.

If this is correct, Saul certainly did not go to Arabia in order to evangelize. He might have been doing what a puzzled zealous prophet might be expected to do: going back to the source to resign his commission.

---

[118] For example, the language of Gal. 3:17-19 is so legalistic in nature that it reads almost like a court transcription.

[119] N. T. Wright, "Paul, Arabia and Elijah," originally published in *Journal of Biblical Literature*, 115:683–692. Accessed on line at http://ntwrightpage.com/Wright_Paul_Arabia_Elijah.pdf.

Alternatively, and perhaps preferably, he might be conceived of as doing what a puzzled, newly commissioned prophet might do, complaining (like Moses, Jeremiah, and others) that he is not able to undertake the work he has been assigned. And whatever still, small voice he may have heard, it was certainly not underwriting the land of zeal in which he had been indulging up until then. His zeal was now to be redirected (Gal. 4:18; see also 2 Cor. 11:2). He was to become the herald of the new king.[120]

With this in mind we can begin to see elements of the dark night of the soul evident in Paul's accounting. Paul's new theology came not through conversations with James (Jesus's brother) or the other followers of the Way, but through "revelation." We can presume, along with Wright, that Paul's trip to Sinai was an introspective time, and a time in which he most likely felt alone and alien to his former Pharisaic Jewish cohort, and a time when God was doing the inner work of re-tooling his thought processes and fundamental beliefs. Through this dark night process Paul went from a dualisitc, self-righteousness to a non-dual and inclusive place of love and acceptance. What a radical transformation! Many of Paul's letters give evidence of his awareness of the unitive path of love. He includes himself with all others and all others with himself in first Corinthians 9:20-22:

> To the Jews I became as a Jew, in order to win Jews. To those under the law, I became as one under the law (though I myself am not under the law) so that I might win those under the law. To those outside the law I became has one outside the law (though I am not free from God's law but am under Christ's law) so that I might win those outside of the law. To the weak, I became weak so that I might win the weak. I have become all things to all people that I might by all means save some.

Paul sees no boundaries or distinctions between classes, religions or peoples. He has become, for all intents and purposes, universalizing in his approach to others. Labels, classes and egoic divisions mean nothing to Paul as a survivor of the dark night. "There is no longer Jew or Greek, there is no longer slave or free, there is no longer male and female, for all of you are one in Christ Jesus." (Gal. 3:28) Paul's many references to the total universalizing nature of his belief provide evidence of the non-dual thinking of transformed spirituality – it is a both/and, a different-and-same type of thinking, just as there are different parts of a body – hands, eyes, feet – they are all part of one body. (1Cor. 12:12)

---

[120] Wright, *Paul, Arabia and Elijah*, 685.

But what is more telltale about Paul's transformation is his claim of having "died to the law" and that "it is no longer 'I' who lives." (Gal. 2:19-20). In terms of the dark night, this means that Paul essentially gave up trying to get it "right" through a perfect obedience to the law. That is an ego-driven quest, and his ego (the 'I' in the statement) has died – literally, he says it has been crucified. As one whose conscious ego has been worked on by the transformative love of God, Paul concludes (like John of the Cross will contend so many years later) that when his spirit (soul) prays, something is happening, but when he prays with his mind (ego) it is thoroughly unfruitful. (1 Cor. 14:14)

Paul's writing is probably the greatest (by sheer volume) single biblical source for the language of transformed spirituality as a result of the inner work of the Divine through the dark night of the soul. Having come face to face with God, Paul fully gets God's power as unconditional love. "For I am convinced that neither death nor life, nor angels, nor rulers, nor things present, nor things to come, nor powers nor height, nor depth, nor anything else in all creation, will be able to separate us from the love of God." (Rom. 8:38-39) Yet through it all he stays totally aware of the fact that, though God will never pull back, his own humanness may get in the way of feeling that presence.

> I do not understand my own actions. For I do not do what I want, but do the very thing I hate. Now if I do what I do not want, I agree that the law is good. But in fact it is no longer that I do it, but the sin that dwells within me. For I know that nothing good dwells within me, that is, in my flesh. I can will what is right, but I cannot do it. For I do not do the good that I want but the evil I do not want is what I do. Now if I do what I do not want, it is no longer I that do it, but sin that dwells within me. (Rom. 7:15-20)

What Paul is saying here, in a language devoid of psychological terms, is that ego (the sin that is in my flesh) still trumps the spirit of his transformed SELF/soul. He recognizes and understands his fallibility and broken humanness as evil (not meaning any personified evil such as the Satan), that is ego, is the great folly of human nature.

Some scholars would also point to Paul's "thorn [that] was given me in the flesh" (2Cor. 12:7) as an example of Paul's on-going dark night. Despite Paul's wish to have it taken away, his understanding that God's power is made manifest in our humanly weakness. In this way Paul is continually reminded, either by his inability to stay the course of transformation or by his nagging irritant that won't go away, that the way of the unitive path with God is a fragile and easily lost state. Transformed souls on the unitive spiritual path, do not suddenly become saint-like models of perfection. Rather, like Paul, they are acutely aware of God's unending out-pouring of unconditional love and how often they (or their egos) can get in the way of experiencing that love. Few have written so eloquently about this as Paul.

Peter, The Most Unlikely Model

Why should we consider Peter in looking at the models of transformation through the dark night of the soul? Peter is the only one who Jesus ever called a devil (Mark 8:33) and he is the only one who is caught in the act of denying his relationship with Jesus (Mark 14:66-72). Almost every time, his first response is wrong or proves how regular and "normal" he was. Even when moved by the sight of his master walking on water, Peter stepped out of the boat and nearly drowned. But that is precisely why he is rightfully included in this list. Peter is the everyman, just another "bloke on the bus" (as my friends in AA would call him). It is his final act of denying his relationship with Jesus that hurls him into the dark night of his soul, and he emerged a few short days later as one who understands the meaning and significance of the empty tomb (John 20:2-8).

Jesus provided a bookend completion ceremony to parallel Peter's denial by asking him three times if Peter loved Jesus and ordained each time with the phrases "Feed my lambs," "Tend my sheep," and "Follow me." (John 21:15-17) Luke then takes up the narrative about Peter's ministry in his account of the Acts of the Apostles. Bumbling Peter, who could never quite get it right, suddenly became the spokesman for the apostles. When the crowds who had gathered in Jerusalem for the festival heard the noise of the wind wherein the disciples had received the holy spirit, and subsequently heard them talking in different native languages, it was Peter who seized the opportunity to speak to the assemblage, and to do so in such a powerful way that thousands were immediately converted to the way.

But the evidence of his transformation comes a bit later in Acts (after the noticeable interlude of the story of Stephen's martyrdom) where we are told of Peter's vision/dream in Acts 10. Peter, a former dualistic and law-abiding Jew, who earlier almost came to blows with Paul over the subject, is told by God in a vision[121] that nothing God had made (rendering it therefore sacred and clean) could be called unclean or profane. Immediately afterward, Peter met with Cornelius and proclaimed, "I truly understand that God shows no partiality, but that in every nation anyone... is acceptable to him." (Acts 10:34) This became the central theme of Peter's ministry from that point on.

---

[121] Visions and revelations are referred to by John of the Cross as the methods God uses in speaking to the soul.

In the two letters attributed to Peter (though most commentaries today dispute Peter's authorship) other examples of universalizing thought are evident. First Peter's theme of equality and love of one another is clear throughout, and his admonition to be awake and aware for the pitfalls that, like a lion, prowl about seeking someone to devour, show his awareness of the dynamic tension between the path of unity and the will of the ego.

Though again we have reason to question Peter's authorship of the Second Letter of Peter, ascribing authorship to Peter (by the editors of the Bible) gives us enough leeway to make some final conclusions about the transformation of the Apostle. What is evident in 2 Peter is the author's awareness of the pitfalls. As I have contended throughout, these authors had no access to psychological terms and often anthropomorphized the will of ego as belonging to Satan or spirits and false prophets. Peter characterizes our will as mere animals whose instincts do not know any better that to do wrong. But he tells the followers that God's love is not simply unconditional, it is patient. "For a thousand years are like a day" to the lord and "the Lord is not slow about his promise." God will come to each believer in exactly the speed that is appropriate to the individual's capability for understanding. Second Peter basically says, stay the course, do your best, and God will be there for you. It is not so much a message of destruction, as many claim (with its references to Sodom and Gomorrah and the great flood), but a message describing the energy that comes from being on the path.

Jesus, and the Ultimate Dark Night Traveler[122]

Thomas Merton described the dark night of the soul as a desert experience, referring to Jesus' time in the desert. Taking that metaphor of the desert, the story of Jesus' ministry could be seen as starting with a dark night type of experience. While only two of the gospels (Matthew and Luke) provide commentary on his 40 days in the desert after his baptism, since Jesus was alone, we are left guessing what actually happened in this dark night experience. In presenting their stories, Matthew (Mt. 4:1-17) and Luke (Lk. 4:1-14) draw from the contemporary mythology of transformation to suggest that Jesus was tempted three times in his desert sojourn. But Mark and John move directly from Jesus' baptism to the start of his ministry, literally suggesting that it began "the next day," (John 1:35) ergo, without the dark night reference.

What provides insight into Jesus' understanding of the dark night are his language, his stories and his parables. Much of the canonical gospels are filled with biography and narrative, and are more concerned with establishing Jesus as the messiah (by showing his miracles and healing) than focusing on his often

---

[122] My goal here will not be to provide the definitive exposé on the teachings of Jesus nor to debate the divinity or humanity of Jesus, but simply to make the case that Jesus' teachings were of the nature of non-dual thinking that is representative of transformed spirituality.

difficult teaching and language of transformation. The gospel of Thomas, however, is simply constructed of what are purported to be the sayings of Jesus and perhaps provides a more distilled view of his teaching.[123] The sayings of Jesus listed in the Gospel of Thomas give an ample array of the type of non-dual thinking that is evident from transformed souls. Logion 4[124] for example reads "Jesus says, 'The man aged in days will not hesitate to ask a little child of seven days about the place of life, and he shall live; for there are many first who shall be last, and they will become one.'" There are many factors in this logion that are counterintuitive. First of all is the fact that circumcision, the Brit Malah, is performed on the eight day; so asking a child of seven days effectively translates to asking not only a preverbal neonate, but more importantly, one who is not yet under the covenant with God. Secondly suggesting that a newborn would know more about the essence of life (the place of life) than a wizened elder seems preposterous. And the logion concludes with an expanded version of the canonical maxim we all know – the last shall be first and the first last – but adds that the first, in being moved to last in line "shall be come one" (other translations read "shall become a single thing").

This logion roughly translates into several key principles representing transformed spirituality. First of all it means that the kingdom of God, and that God itself cannot be held as a thought. It exists before language or thought and before any ritual classifies or sanctifies it. But equally as important is the concept that God levels the playing field; that the last and first are made indistinguishable; that no preference is given to anyone; and, in fact, some exegetes contend, the reference to being made one is to the division between male and female is eliminated.

But perhaps the most obvious of the logions is Logion 22:

When you make the two one,
and when you make the inside as the outside,
and the outside as the inside,
and the upper as the lower,
and when you make the male and the female into a single one,
so that the male is not male and the female not female,

---

[123] Bourgeault, *Wisdom Jesus*, 54-55.

[124] Thomas refers to each saying with the term "logion," a Greek word for saying or aphorism. All citations of the Gospel of Thomas are taken from http://www.earlychristianwritings.com/thomas/ produced by Peter Kirby, 2012.

and when you make eyes in place of an eye,
and a hand in place of a hand,
and a foot in place of a foot,
an image in place of an image,
then shall you enter.

Only one who has moved past dualistic thinking could conceive such logic let alone string a series together like this. I do not think Jesus meant only when one is able to create life or regenerate limbs will one be able to enter into the kingdom of God. Rather he seems to be indicating that it takes this type of unitive, non-dual thinking to be able to see God in the first place. "This kind of reunification can only happen once we have transcended the egoic operating system. Once one reaches the causal point where all forms converge in oneness (and in this Gospel Jesus frequently refers to that point as "the light"), immediately the grand dance of manifestation begins all over again."[125]

Many of Jesus' parables contain equally baffling non-dualities. I want to point out just three of the over 40 parables told by Jesus: The Good Samaritan, The Prodigal Son and the Wicked Tenants. In the Good Samaritan Parable, Jesus uses reverse logic to point out that actions are more important that professions of faith. The one who was a "good neighbor" in the story was a member of a despised and outcaste tribe – Samaritans were treated like dogs. Yet despite being of this sub-human group, he showed more mercy that the Levite or Pharisee.

In my youth the parable of the Prodigal son had always bothered me. I identified with the older "good" brother standing out in the field shouting, "Hey, what about me?" So very many sermons have been preached about this parable but most focus on the repentant nature of the son or on the compassion of God that forgives our errant ways when and if we are repentant. But the significant element of the story is that the father did not know that the son was repenting. It says that "while the son was still a long way off," the father saw him and ran out to greet him, wrapping him in his cloak. This is a radical level of forgiveness that is unwarranted and given even before the sin is confessed. It cannot be comprehended by the dualistic mind that seeks justice for the good and punishment for the bad.

The third parable I would point to is referred to as the parable of the Wicked Tenants and is found in Mt. 21:33-44. A landowner who had planted vineyards left for another country and rented his house to some tenants and when the harvest time came, he sent his servants to help with the harvest. The tenants beat the servants and sent them away. So the landowner sent even more servants,

---

[125] Borgeault, *Wisdom*, 57.

who, likewise were beaten and thrown out. Finally he sent his son thinking that surely the tenants would respect his son. But the tenants, thinking that they could steal the inheritance, killed the landowner's son. Jesus then turned the story over to the crowd asking them how the landowner should treat the tenants, and the unanimous verdict is death! But in response Jesus pulls out a Psalm (118, v. 22) and tells the people that the rejected stone is the one the mason will use as the corner stone! What? Why? In each of these parables, Jesus points out that the unlikely person will be the recipient of blessings. Two gospel accounts of the parable of the feast show us that it is not the invited who get to come to the banquet, but all others – "Go out into the highways and byways" and invite everyone in. In the Beatitudes, Jesus points to the way of love and healing: the meek will inherit the earth (not just a prize, a reward or a plot of land – they get the entire planet), the hungry will be filled (but those who are full will be sent away), and "blessed are you when people revile you and persecute you and utter all kinds of evil against you falsely on my account. Rejoice and be glad for your reward is great." (Mt. 5:3-12) Frequently Jesus makes mention of the way of the cross, or that the way to gain life is to lose your life. "Unless a grain of wheat falls to the earth and dies it remains a single grain; but if it dies, it bears much fruit." (Jn. 12:24)

This reverse logic is just a way of pushing the thinking of his followers – like the Buddhist teacher's use of a koan – to the breaking point, where dualism can no longer exist and non-dualism takes over. In non-dual thinking, Jesus could say things like "I am in all things and all things are in me," "I and the father are one," "Split a piece of wood and I am there, pick up a rock and you will find me there." Bourgeault summarizes this logic by saying,

> Seeing Jesus through this new filter is both profoundly unsettling and profoundly helpful: unsettling, because it dislodges us even further from our 20/20 hindsight– And lingering smugness that we have Jesus teachings in our hip pocket. But joyous in the same sense that our heart knows this already; and profoundly joyous because the spaciousness emerging from this new portrait gives us the freedom to go deeper.[126]

So clearly we see evidence of the transformed thinking of Jesus, but what of his dark nights? We note that there are several references to Jesus going off alone to pray and spending all night praying (Mt. 14:23, MK. 1:35, and Lk. 6:12). Jesus admitted (Jn 12:27) that his "soul was troubled." But he recognized that he needed to stay troubled because that was where the growth happened.

---

[126] Bourgeault, *Wisdom Jesus*, 61.

Jesus' final dark night came on the night of his arrest, in the Garden at Gethsemane. Not only was it actually night but it was perhaps the darkest hour of his life. Though no one was awake to witness it, we can imagine that he prayed to be spared the "cup of poison" and the pain of crucifixion. I can only presume that the authors (Matthew, Mark and Luke) wanted to give us an actual example of the grief in the dark night, as if to say that Jesus, in sharing humanity with us, also shared this darkest of nights as well. John, however, who allegedly was one of the three disciples who went further into the garden with Jesus and may have had a chance to hear the prayer, provides a wholly different prayer in the garden. But, beyond the prayers of the dark night, when it came down to his final hours, Jesus showed how clearly he had become master of the dark night. Throughout his "trial" he responded to accusations or questions from his non-dual point of view. And when he was crucified, he turned to chanting the Psalms as a method for being with the pain and darkness.[127]

Jesus' short three-year ministry is thus bookended by the dark night from fasting and meditating in the desert to the ordeals of his last hours. The model he set was a model of wisdom salvation that comes from being outcast and downtrodden. He never exalted the good and well-heeled but always lifted up the poor, the sinners, the widows and the children. His examples were Samaritans, tax collectors and even prostitutes. His teachings were clearly of a non-dual nature and speak to the fact that he had gone through the sloughing off of the ego that permits one to live and act with that kind of compassion. His path was one of seeking to be present and in the moment at all times. If we look at the Jesus model from a purely human perspective, he was clearly a transformed spirit. And if we consider Jesus as divine, we get a clear example of what the unitive path of love in God produces in personal and human terms.

Thus the Bible is filled with examples of the type of transformation resulting from the dark night of the soul. Its authors see the darkness as a time of transformation. They regularly use a dark cloud to obscure the image and essence of God as unknowable and keep their reader off-balance with key teachings that are counterintuitive and puzzling. But if John of the Cross is correct in his assertion that the scriptures are filled with "so many passages" that we would never have enough time and space to write about them all, it falls on us to identify them at least by the nature and theme. This chapter has covered a few of themes we might recognize from some of the more prominent characters and stories of transformation in the Bible (as I see them):

---

[127] The words heard spoken by Jesus while on the cross follow sequence as though he may have been reciting the Psalms in order: Psalm 22:1 "My God, My God why have you forsaken me?" Ps. 22:15 "I am thirsty." Ps. 31:5 "Into your hands, I commend my spirit."

- Biblical references to the transformed effect of such experiences are marked by name changes, protracted absences (during which we have to presume that something mysterious is happening), and by making the character totally unrecognizable to his/her most intimate friends and family.
- John of the Cross often refers to the use of visions, dreams and revelations (supernatural apprehensions) as the inner workings of God/holy spirit on the soul.[128] While not directly covered in this chapter, revelation, when viewed from the point of view of the dark night, comes as a challenging *non sequitur* to the life and beliefs of the character (vis a vis, the apostle Peter's revelation that all things created by God are holy and therefore clean).
- The grief and suffering caused by a simple longing for God shifts the writers' context from reliance on an intervening God of solutions to acceptance of God's way as *the* way.
- The dark night of the soul can transform even the most unlikely of heroes into the wizened leader revered by others. So many of the stories in the Hebrew Bible follow that theme while Saul/Paul is perhaps the quintessential example from the Christian Bible.
- Finally, the transformed (non-dual and counterintuitive) wisdom of the character is perhaps the most common theme we see in these stories. Characters like David, Jacob/Israel, Saul/Paul who originally held onto an eye-for-an-eye logic and prayed to a warrior/conqueror God, speak in terms of acceptance and inclusion that hold both good and bad together in the one after their transformation.

None of these interpretations however have come from the use of exegetical texts but are reworked by attempting, as John of the Cross did, to view them through the lens of the dark night of the soul. Perhaps one reason people who experience the dark night report feeling so alone is that the dark night is not well understood by their peers and contemporaries. Certainly few if any of the scriptural characters had a language to describe what happened, and only Jesus seems to refer to the requirements necessary for one to enter onto the path of spiritual transformation (e.g., dying to oneself, taking up a cross (a humiliating death), entering as a child, and so on).

In the following chapters we see how this the dark night is experienced by contemporary individuals on that path; how they describe their changes in faith, their relationship with God and the difficulties they encountered in dealing with a

---

[128] John of the Cross, *Ascent*, 226-252.

process that at the same time is gut-wrenchingly real and yet defies any traditional verbal description. Each describes the incomprehensible loneliness of their faith journey. But as we shall see, the path itself may look and sound completely different for each individual; as a result of the precipitating impasse, as a result of the individuals heritage, previous religion and theological understanding, and as a result of the degree of the individual attachment to, or resistance to letting go of, his/her preconceived notions of the Divine, oneself and the relationship between.

**Chapter Three – Wrestling the Angel:
Personal accounts of the dark night of the soul**

No one is ever prepared to endure the long silence that follows intimacy. No one is prepared to face it when it comes after lovemaking. No one is prepared to face it when it comes after a season of intimacy with God. It is the hardest thing to talk about, and it is the hardest thing in the spiritual journey to prepare for. The long silence between intimacies, the interminable pause between words, the immeasurable seconds between pulses, the quiet between epiphanies, the hush after ecstasy, the listening for God – this is the spiritual journey, learning how to live in the meantime, between the last time you heard from God and the next you hear from God.[129]

Renita Weems

However difficult it may be, finding words to describe the ebb and flow of spirituality is a challenge not only of many spiritual seekers, it is particularly difficult on those whose career and calling are focused on the spiritual side of life. Having experienced a calling to the ministry does not exempt one from experiencing dry spells or the long silence of which Weems talks (in fact for many, it seems to launch one on to the path). But the dry spells do seem to be more threatening and perhaps the recovery from them can seem even shakier for those in the profession. Yet simultaneously these periods of longing, these seasons of silence, often mark a deepening of one's faith and result in opening more fully to the Divine. John of the Cross' description of the process of the dark night of the soul provides the reader with a framework. But what is missing is a way to understand the actual feelings associated with the night passage. How would one describe what is happening or what has happened in the dark night of the soul? This chapter explores the shape and feel of the dark night of the soul as experienced by a few autobiographers, each "religious" in her own right. The cast of characters includes:

- Mother Teresa of Calcutta, whose letters to her confessor were chronicled by Brian Kolodiejchuk (*Come Be My Light*), was a nun who founded the order of the Missionaries of Mercy and who spent her life ministering to the dying poor of Calcutta, India. Because of

---

[129] Weems, *Listening for God*, 25.

her mission and the pervasiveness of death and dying around her, Teresa often felt that God was distant and deaf to her constant prayer.

- Renita Weems, whose book, *Listening For God* provides the opening quote for the chapter, is a biblical scholar and ordained minister. Her book is a chronicle of a crisis of faith as experienced by a minister whose very job was in jeopardy when the well went dry.
- Karen Armstrong has been described as a theological anthropologist. A former nun turned English Literature professor, Armstrong's spiritual journey as a result of dealing with severe epilepsy, *The Spiral Staircase*, is a look at the dark night as precipitated by physical/emotional trauma.

What these authors provide is a rich tapestry of language used in describing the experience of the dark night of the soul. Whereas John of the Cross has outlined a vocabulary that has been used for centuries by (especially Catholic) spiritual directors, the three authors describe the experiences in their own words, using their available metaphors and applying it all to the life events as they unravel for them. While I chose these three authors for their specific references to the dark night of the soul, what I am attempting to show with these accounts is the incredibly wide array of descriptions of how the dark night feels, is perceived and is eventually thought of by those who experience it. Were one not looking for references to the process and dynamic, much of what each has written about may pass unrecognized as dark night, or if recognized as such, may appear as totally different from what John of the Cross was describing.

Though the three authors being reviewed here are only a few of the many from whom I might have chosen, they represent several common threads:

- Each described their dark nights as a time of deep sadness and despair
- Each one talked at length of the fruitless nature of their prayer life and of the pain of longing to hear from God when nothing was forthcoming
- Though each represents a different type of onset of the dark night, each one spoke of the sense of absence of the Divine or of the contrast between the former felt presence and the clear awareness of God's absence
- But what is most clear is that each person emerged from her dark night with a deeper connection with the Divine

What is clearly most similar among these authors is their unshakable belief in God; that is, that God actually existed in some way that was unquestionable, yet appeared to each as "on-again-off-again," or as Armstrong puts it, that it may often be that God was "conspicuous by his absence from my life."[130] Similarly, both Weems wrote of her long periods of silence, and Mother Teresa talked of her "terrible sense of loss – this untold darkness – this loneliness – this continual longing for God."[131] So let us begin there.

Mother Teresa of Calcutta

Mother Teresa's story seems the logical place to begin as it is based in her many descriptions of a deep-seated love for Jesus and her desire to serve him. Entering the convent at eighteen (in 1928) the young Gonxha Agnes Bojaxhuia, who took the spiritual name of Mary Teresa (after St. Theresa of Lisieux), already knew she had been called to serve the poor. She wrote that from the time of 5 ½ when she was baptized, she knew she had been called to save others' souls and specifically the souls of the poor. Thus, at her request, she was transferred to India after only her first year. In her early writings and letters, Teresa talked passionately of her love of Jesus and of being his "spouse." Her personal vow was to refuse him nothing – she would give everything she had, and every moment of her life to being the love of Jesus for others. She yearned to be a perfect reflection of the love she felt from Jesus.

While her early work in India was serving the poor, it was to take a radical turn many years later (in late 1946) when she heard the voice of Jesus call her into deeper service to minister to the poorest of the poor – the sick and dying and forgotten poor in Calcutta's ghettos. It was a dangerous calling and when she presented it to her superiors, it was flatly refused. Teresa continued pleading her case – with all of the fervor of one who has such a spiritual call – over the coming years until it was finally granted and she set up her convent house just outside the city of Calcutta. The sisters, irrespective of their nationality, were to become Indian in every aspect and to adhere to full poverty. "They will all think me mad – after so many years – to begin a thing which will bring me for the most part only suffering – but He calls me."[132] Teresa was convinced that it was not her who would be doing the work. In her mind, she was nothing – a tool, a pawn to be used by God in his service. Teresa was driven to serve her spouse, Jesus, and to him she had surrendered completely.

Teresa kept hearing and seeing "voices and visions" during the time she was making her case to do Jesus' bidding. She detailed several of the conversations and visions (dreams) in her letters to her superiors. She seemed

---

[130] Karen Armstrong, *The Spiral Staircase, My Climb Out of Darkness* (New York: Random House, 2004), 43.

[131] Brian Kolodiejchuk, *Mother Teresa: Come Be My Light* (New York: Doubleday, 2007), 1.

[132] Kolodiejchuk, *Mother Teresa*, 54.

resolute to do this work until shortly after she had launched her order, the Missionaries of Charity. Teresa recounts that day:

> Today I learned a good lesson – the poverty of the poor must be often so hard for them. I went rounding looking for a home - I walked and walked till my legs and my arms ached. I thought how they must also ache in body and soul looking for home - food - help. The temptation grew strong - the palace buildings of Loreto came rushing into my mind - all the beautiful things and comforts - the people they mix with - in a word everything. "You have only to say the word and all that will be yours again," the tempter kept saying to me... I did not let a single tear come... Even if I suffer more than now - I still want to do Your Holy will. This is the dark night of the birth of the Society. My God give me courage now - this moment - to persevere in following Your call.[133]

But Loreto was not as willing to have her back as her temptations might have had her believe. In fact, shortly thereafter the Mother Superior of Loreto convent forbade any contact between her nuns and the Sisters of Teresa's order. It was hard work with death literally around every corner. Her spiritual director advised her not to continue but her work could not be denied. Over the years of daily ministering to the dying poor of Calcutta, Teresa's voices began to fade. For years she had been hearing Jesus tell her "I thirst" which she understood to be his thirst for the love of souls she encountered. But gradually the voice was replaced by darkness devoid of Jesus's voice. Teresa traced the onset of her dark night back to right after she began her work in the ghettos.

Teresa's inner darkness increased over the years and seemed to be heightened by the publicity she and her order of nuns were getting. Having others praise her efforts only made the longing to hear God more painful. She wrote, "The longing for God is terribly painful yet the darkness is becoming greater. The pain is so great that I really don't feel anything for all the publicity and the talk of the people."[134] Much of the dissonance she felt stemmed from how she understood her relationship with God through Jesus. In her mind she was nothing and yet God had chosen her – called her – to do this horrifying work. Her innocence faded and dried up and she felt torn between an unshakable calling to be the light of Christ to the forgotten people of the world and her personal need to be reassured that she was the beloved spouse of her chosen life partner.

---

[133] Kolodiejchuk, *Mother Teresa*, 133-34.

[134] Kolodiejchuk, *Mother Teresa*, 174.

The darkness is so dark – and I am alone. Unwanted. Forsaken. The loneliness of the heart that wants love is unbearable. Where is my faith? My God, how painful is this unknown pain. It pains without ceasing. I have no faith. I dare not utter the words and thoughts that crowd my heart and make me suffer untold agony… When I try to raise my thoughts to Heaven there is such convicting emptiness that those very thoughts return like sharp knives and hurt my very soul. Love – the word – brings me nothing. I am told God loves me – and yet the reality of darkness and coldness and emptiness is so great that nothing touches my soul.[135]

These thoughts embarrassed Mother Teresa and when her spiritual director was being transferred she quickly wrote him a note begging him to destroy all of her letters. But even in her deepest darkness, she never questioned her unity with God. Her longing for God and love of God were both the grounding of her faith and the origin of her ordeal.[136]

In the midst of her darkest hour, Teresa caught a glimpse of what it all meant. She suddenly realized that on the cross Jesus was alone and feeling forsaken. For years she had prayed to know Jesus and suddenly in her pain, torment and aloneness, she felt the touch of Jesus. "Today really I felt a deep joy – that Jesus can't go anymore through the agony – but that He wants to go through it in me. More than ever I surrender myself to him. – Yes – more than ever I will be at His disposal."[137] She began finding spiritual joy from her internal struggles and spoke often of the joy of having nothing, of having absolute poverty – the poverty of the cross. And in that she found what ultimately could be called her mission statement. She wrote, "If ever I become a saint, I will surely be one of 'darkness.' I will continually be absent from heaven – to light the light of those in darkness on earth."[138]

Looking back on her dark night experience, Mother Teresa had to admit that she really never had doubt. Once she had surrendered to God's will, there was no turning back – "though it may mean the death of you. The conviction comes the moment you surrender. Then there is no doubt." Teresa had indeed become one with Jesus through her painful ordeal of darkness. She identified with his pain and suffering, with his moment in Gethsemane of not wanting the cup, with his loneliness on the cross. She had crossed over from a young girl in

[135] Kolodiejchuk, *Mother Teresa*, 187.

[136] Kolodiejchuk, *Mother Teresa*, 203.

[137] Kolodiejchuk, *Mother Teresa*, 215.

[138] Kolodiejchuk, *Mother Teresa*, 230.

love with her master to a selfless instrument of the outpouring of God's love and in doing so had become the perfect reflection of Jesus she had prayed for as a young nun. It was, for her, the death of wanting that was so painful and when that was illuminated for what it was, and she could let it go, her joy returned. "I am at his disposal," she wrote to her long time friend Eileen Egan, "He can do with me as it pleaseth Him, without even a thought of consulting me. I want to be his little one, if He so wants, otherwise I will be happy to be just nothing and He everything."[139] In total, Mother Teresa's dark night of the soul lasted for nearly 10 years and was virtually continual during that time. For Teresa, Jesus was answering her prayer and making her understand the suffering and loneliness of the poor as only Jesus could understand it.

Reverend Renita J. Weems

Reverend Weems presents a different case. Renita grew up in the world of Southern Baptist revivals and storefront African-American Pentecostal "Bible" churches. She recalls with warm nostalgia how she would go to Sunday afternoon story-telling sessions where the older men of the church, many of whom could not even read, sat around telling embellished stories from the Bible. It was not theology but is was real and captivating. But what really captured her has a young teenager were the revival shows. These self-proclaimed preachers were part magician, part showmen but totally captivating. She was curious and attracted at the same time, and it was that wonder that drew her into her pursuit of theology.

But the spiritual highs she once experienced under the tent and the fascination with the made up stories from the Bible quickly faded under the scrutiny of her theological studies. Religion became academic – a subject to be mastered, dissected and lectured about. And, almost without noticing it, one day she realized the luster had faded and the excitement was gone. "How does a minister admit that she hasn't heard from God in a long, long time? It is much easier and safer to talk about the springtime of faith, when the desire for inward journeying is a insatiable and belief in a ministry is irrepressible."[140]

The metaphor of seasons seemed to fit Renita's experience. "Seasons are not stages. They are neither linear nor chartable. They do not begin and end at predictable times."[141] Likewise her experiences of God seemed to cycle through seasons – times of spiritual highs followed by periods of nothingness and

---

[139] Kolodiejchuk, *Mother Teresa*, 284.

[140] Weems, *Listening for God*, 26.

[141] Weems, *Listening for God*, 31.

dormancy. "I have lost my faith of thousand times, only to find it 999 times. Belief in mystery has waned and reappeared repeatedly throughout the journey. This on-again, off-again love affair with the sacred is unnerving. But it is, oddly enough, also fascinating."[142] At first this appeared as something she needed to fix. How could she regain the highs or program out the lows? Through it all she continued to pray and even when the prayer was dry and senseless, she prayed the prayer she could until she could pray the prayer she wanted, and in doing so her prayer life shifted. "Prayer is not so much learning to write or talk to someone or some presence outside yourself as becoming mindful of a conversation already taking place deep inside."[143]

Her spiritual life became a series of what she called "stalking epiphanies," trying to find something that would bring back the excitement she once felt. Otherwise, she feared that she would be exposed as a fraud by her classes or her parishioners. Though there seemed to be a pattern to her spirituality – that any spiritual high point was followed by a period of low – the truly unnerving part was that in all honesty her spirituality was suffering and not at all what she felt would be sufficient to sustain her in her roles of minister, theological researcher, writer and professor. "It never occurred to me, because no one ever told me, that I would one day as a minister stop believing; stop believing in God as I once had, stop believing in the religion I have been practicing most of my life, stop believing in what I was doing, stop believing that my life as a minister, professor of Bible and writer made any sense. Had I been warned that this day was coming, I might have been more careful... But I didn't know."[144]

The religion of her origin was one that preached of angels and a fierce and jealous God. It was a religion that was serious salvation for a people in captivity. For her people and their ancestors, whose history of slavery and exile allowed them to identify with the ancient Jews, the Bible made sense in their lives. But Weems' life was different than that of oppressed former slaves living in a still-segregated south. "I and those of my generation probably don't believe in God, in angels, and even in miracles the way our ancestors did. We need a God who is not squeamish about disclosing the Divine self in a thoroughly secular world and in the midst of ordinary daily existence, speaking to us through the noise of our hopeless routines and willing to touch us in our carnal places.

---

[142] Weems, *Listening for God*, 30.

[143] Weems, *Listening for God*, 62.

[144] Weems, *Listening for God*, 38.

We need a God who has more of a sense of humor than did our ancestors about what exactly constitutes prayer."[145]

As her career progressed, Weems encountered young students who reminded her of her youthful innocence. She was presented with challenging questions that forced her to take a deeper look at her own understanding of the relationship between God and God's creatures. She came to see God as a great communicator, teaching her how to gently handle the language and lessons of spirituality. Spirituality happened more in the spaces in between than in what one knew or about which one could preach. "As with most great communicators, God knows that the point of silence and the pause between sentences is not to give the audience the chance to fill the silence with empty babbling but to help create more depth to the conversation."[146]

After a period of time, the gaps began to make sense as a part of the process. It was like anything in nature – sometimes the farmer needs to let the field lay in fallow in order to restore its ability to grow new crops. Sometimes one needs to rest, wait and allow the body to catch up with the mind. Or better yet, let the body gear *down* to the soul's pace."[147] But what was still missing for Weems was a way to get back in connection with the God of her understanding – to find the juice that once sparked her and set her off on this journey of faith to begin with. And for that she felt that she was at a distinct disadvantage.

Let's face it: there's nothing exotic about being a Methodist minister and ex-Pentecostal who is now married to a Baptist preacher. Nothing exotic about it at all. No wonder I haven't heard a word from God. What do Pentecostals, Methodists, or Baptist know about the deeper more subtle mysteries of the spiritual journey? I lack the scaffolding for building up my spiritual life. Look at what I've been missing in these traditions. No incense. No chants. No saints. No beads. No icons. No heroes dressed up in baroque headgear and ostentatious robes. And worst of all, no liturgy to speak of. Low church, free church, whatever – any tradition that tries to sell God as right here visible, on the verge of appearing any minute right before your eyes without any genuflecting on our part is an inferior church. Everyone knows that if you want the inside scoop and to discover the secrets of prayer you must read the Catholics.[148]

[145] Weems, *Listening for God*, 51.

[146] Weems, *Listening for God*, 62.

[147] Weems, *Listening for God*, 73.

[148] Weems, *Listening for God*, 102-103.

The truth for Weems was to appear through the struggle to find meaning on her own. The church of her origin had set her up with expectations of God that she now found unreal or unrealistic in the light of her advanced studies, but the other truth that was so apparent for her was that there still was something there – out there and in her – that was undeniable. She felt that she had to drop all of her previously held expectations of how God *should* be in order to experience how God *wishes* to be manifest for her. "Institutional religion has both blessed me and injured me by handing me some expectations about God that I can test out. Thankfully, God confirmed some of those expectations. Thankfully, God ignored a great many of those expectations. But it was both in confirming a few and ignoring a great many other of my expectations that God offered me a chance for inner discovery and growth."[149]

Weems equates her discovery process to Moses and the Israelites fleeing Pharaoh's armies. Arriving at the Red Sea (or Reed Sea), what seems to be an insurmountable task, Moses cried out to God for help and God's response took them by surprise. God literally tells Moses to instruct the people just to step forward. The path is always right there before you – out there in the deep water – it's just that you cannot see it until you step forward. "Those who wish to find themselves must first be willing to lose themselves. Only when we risk getting lost do we find our way, and only when we stop trying to see our footsteps does our pathway become more certain."[150]

For Weems the seasons of winter – her dark nights – never really went away. They kept recurring. Often she would be tempted "to walk away, give up, stop praying, stop believing, curse the winter, and withdraw"[151] but she never has. Each trip through, each season, has yielded deeper insights and a fuller relationship with God. Her spiritual practice of prayer was never dropped – even when it seemed dry and fruitless. She noticed that sometimes those practices that made the least sense are the ones that kept her anchored in faith and facing the right direction. Like so many others on this trip, Weems discovered that she could not have God on her terms. She must be willing to meet God on God's terms. She mused at one point, "So exactly what have I had in mind all these months and years when I contemplated about God being silent? What exactly did I want God to talk with me about? What was on my mind? American slavery? The Holocaust? Why newborns die? It's as though God pulled up a chair in my

---

[149] Weems, *Listening for God*, 104.

[150] Weems, *Listening for God*, 121.

[151] Weems, *Listening for God*, 166.

75

kitchen and said, 'Why don't we begin with forgiveness?' No. No. No. Not forgiveness. Anything but forgiveness."[152]

Her great discovery was that she had wanted all of the gifts, "all the benefits of the inner journey without any of the responsibilities that came along with that. I wanted God to speak to me, but I didn't want God to confront me."[153] And on the inward journey toward God, one is always confronted with this reality: all of one's previously held beliefs and all expectations of God and placed on God must be dispensed with, dashed to the ground, in order to make space for that which God has in store for us.

> To grow and to adapt in light of changing circumstances and changing seasons; we stumble upon doors we didn't know where there; we grope for light we barely make out; and some*where* in the process of it all, some*where* between laughing and crying, as we look back at all the *wheres* our stubborn, frightened self has been, we make out some meaning and direction to our life, not of our own making but of someone else's making, someone more intelligent, yes, but also someone with an infinitely better sense of humor than we have.[154]

Renita Weems writes from a depth of faith that was hard won, but one that is both rich and sustaining. She no longer fears the winter seasons because her experience is that there always is a spring that follows. It is just that sometimes what we know gets in the way of what we can experience. As the great historian and mythologist, Joseph Campbell noted:

> The question sometimes arises as to whether the experience of mystery and transcendence is more available to those who have undergone some kind of religious and spiritual training, for whom, it has all been named completely. It may be less available to them precisely because they have got it all named in the book. One way to deprive yourself of an experience is indeed to expect it. Another is a have a name for it before you have the experience.[155]

Karen Armstrong

Thus far we have looked at the dark night that was precipitated by the gravity of a life in service to the suffering and one that was precipitated by

---

[152] Weems, *Listening for God*, 172.

[153] Weems, *Listening for God*, 172.

[154] Weems, *Listening for God*, 96.

[155] Joseph Campbell, *Thou Art That: Transforming Religious Metaphor* (Novato CA: New World Library, 2001), 13.

having overly inspected the mystery. In Karen Armstrong, we find a third possible origin of the dark night experience: one that is precipitated by an event. Armstrong had begun her search to find God as a nun in London, but shortly after her entry into the convent she started having seizures and fainting spells. Her battle with an undiagnosed case of epilepsy resulted not only in years of depression, being incorrectly diagnosed (and hospitalized) as mentally ill, but also her expulsion from the convent and eventually the loss of her second career in education. It ultimately crushed her belief in the existence of God.

Ms. Armstrong's depression (the result of her mistreatment by the medical community) had led her to a nearly fatal suicide attempt. Shortly thereafter she explained to a friend, "I really couldn't make religion work for me. I really tried. I tried to pray, to meditate, but I never got anywhere. The real test is when you try to find God on your own, without props, without beautiful music, singing and spectacle, when there is just you on your knees. And I could never do that. I wanted to believe it all; I wanted to have an encounter with God, but I never did. God was never a reality for me. I just don't believe that God is there."[156]

But what sustained Armstrong through all of her early adulthood and first two careers was her academic prowess and intense study of literature. Not long after leaving Oxford, she was asked by a friend to appear on a talk show – mostly as a result of having just published an autobiographical exposé of her life in the convent (*Through The Narrow Gate*). While the BBC episode was not much to speak of, it did bring Karen into the light as a brilliant extemporaneous speaker ("embarrassingly good" the producer had commented), and was to vault her into a different world than she had ever imagined. Karen was asked to work on a BBC, Channel 4, production of *The First Christian*, a series on Jesus and Paul. The work sent her to Israel under the direction of a Jewish/Israeli producer.

It was on this trip that Karen rediscovered a love for the sacred. From the landscape to the many holy sites the crew used as backdrops for the series, Karen was immersed in the reality of the people and cultures that shaped early theology. Often her conversations with her Jewish producer resulted in new insights as he casually quipped that Judaism had no real theology. It caused her to question her own beliefs "How could you live your faith unless you were convinced that God existed? How could you live a Christian life if you could not accept the official doctrines about Jesus?"[157] His answer was simply that it was an "orthopraxy instead of orthodoxy;" right doing instead of right beliefs, and it was a truth she had always felt. The rigid belief structure she had held before

---

[156] Armstrong, *Spiral Staircase*, 130
[157] Armstrong, *Spiral Staircase*, 236.

entering the convent started crumbling. Armstrong immersed herself in trying to understand the real Paul and how very Jewish both he and Jesus were in all of what they did. With the help of her Israeli host, she came to understand Talmudic law and saw the questions put to Jesus by the Pharisees not as a test to trip him up but as the standard practice of worship of the people. And through it all she saw "increasingly, Judaism and Christianity seemed to be one faith tradition which had gone in two different directions."[158] She saw with compassion the daily plight of people torn apart by those two (or as she later would uncover, three) directions, and something opened up inside.

Her work on Paul, *The First Christian*, though not highly acclaimed, led to another program on *The Crusades*. Studying the crusades intensely in preparation for this next series sent her back to Israel. She uncovered the immense societal hatred that resulted from not understanding another's beliefs. Working on *The Crusades* was earth-shattering for Karen and she began to question the Christian perspective she had always held, "If we had cultivated a vicious hatred of both Judaism and Islam for so many centuries, what other mistakes had we made and what other misapprehensions had we nurtured?"[159] The work was intense but her passion for it rose to the occasion, so that when BBC lost funding for the project, she was left in the lurch and felt something she had never expressed before. Because of the repression of the convent lifestyle and the subsequent repression of all emotions by the drugs given to her as a result of her misdiagnoses, Karen had never felt pain like this. Now with her condition under control she was finally able to feel and express emotions as they came up – her heart had begun to thaw and she suddenly could feel the pain of other people. "I was very angry, and though my rage may have seemed negative to friends who tried to talk me out of it, it was actually an advance. And, although I did not know this at the time, because the ability to experience pain and sorrow is the *sine qua non* of enlightenment, my spiritual quest could begin."[160]

The cancellation of the project released Karen to consider what she might do next. Because of the exposure she had to each of the Abrahamic religions, she felt a new passion to write and decided to write about God. The *History of God* would be a peeling back of the shrouds masking the commonalities behind the three monotheistic religions. It was a quest that ultimately returned her to a belief in God. After many, many years of darkness and disbelief, some light seemed to

---

[158] Armstrong, *Spiral Staircase*, 244.

[159] Armstrong, *Spiral Staircase*, 257.

[160] Armstrong, *Spiral Staircase*, 262-263.

be dawning for her. "There was no sudden road-to-Damascus illumination, and it was only in retrospect that I realized that the decision to write about God had been a defining moment."[161] Though friends and agents would try to discourage her, Karen had found her passion and rediscovered her own path.

> The great myths show that when you follow somebody else's path, you go astray. The hero has to set off by himself, leaving the old world and the old ways behind. He must venture into the darkness of the unknown, where there is no map and no clear route. He must fight his own monsters, not somebody else's, explore his own labyrinth, and endure his own ordeal before he can find what is missing in his life.

> When I entered my convent, I thought I had embarked on a mystical adventure like that of Percival and the other Knights of the Grail, but instead of finding my own path I had to follow somebody else's. Instead of striking out on my own, I had conformed to a way of life and modes of thought that had often seemed alien. As a result, I found myself in a wasteland, an inauthentic existence, in which I struggled mightily but fruitlessly to do what I was told.[162]

Armstrong had finally found her way back to the beginning only in the process she had been transformed. She had rediscovered her belief in and appreciation for mystery and most importantly she had discovered her own God – the God of her own understanding. In the end religion had something of value to offer. She found that she did not have to reject the church in order to enjoy this freedom to believe. "The myths and laws of religion are not true because they conform to some metaphysical, scientific, or historical reality but because they are life enhancing. But you will not discover their truth unless you apply these myths and doctrines to your own life and put them into practice... In the course of my studies, I have discovered that the religious quest is not about discovering 'the truth' or 'the meaning of life' but about living as intensely as possible here and now."[163]

Karen Armstrong discovered that she had to embody the two essential elements of religion before she could regain her faith: she had to set off on her own path and she had to acknowledge her own pain and feel it fully. In her studies of multiple religions, Armstrong has found that all religions place

---

[161] Armstrong, *Spiral Staircase*, 265.

[162] Armstrong, *Spiral Staircase*, 268-69.

[163] Armstrong, *Spiral Staircase*, 270-71.

suffering "on the top of their agenda because it is an inescapable fact of human life."[164] More importantly if one denies one's own pain it becomes easier to dismiss the pain and suffering of others. "Every single one of the major traditions… teaches a spirituality of empathy, by means of which you relate your own suffering to that of others."[165]

Armstrong was able to look back at her life not as a series of failures but as a life lived by trying to use someone else's theology, and that can never work for long. Like so many on this path of the dark night, Karen Armstrong found that the pain and darkness broke her open and that the opening led to the discovery of true compassion. Compassion, she notes, is not always the popular choice of virtues as it leads to actually understanding those that others might label as enemies. "But I have myself found that compassion is a habit of mind that is transforming. The science of compassion which guides my studies has changed the way I experience the world."[166] The transformative path and the practice of compassion, she notes, is not always comfortable. "But this pain is a small price to pay for the spirituality of empathy. Paradoxically, what I have gained from this identification with suffering is joy. This is something that I did not expect."[167]

Armstrong's journey through the dark night lasted even longer than Mother Teresa's – all totaled over 20 years. Its darkest nights were not induced by her spiritual quest but rather a result of a neurological disorder. Others we encounter are thrown into the darkness through divorce or calamity, as is my own case. However, the dark night experience is not ever about the situation that precipitates it, nor as we shall later see, is the experience of God on the other side of the night ever a story of rescue from the normal pains of a life lived.

Personal Connection with the Dark Night Experience

Reading the personal accounts of these three authors, I can identify with bits and pieces of each and it may be helpful at this juncture to add in a bit of my own narrative. I grew up in a Lutheran household and as such, steeped in the "truths" of Martin Luther's *Small Catechism* and *Large Catechism*, each assertion of which would end with the statement, "This is most certainly true." Our family sang loudly and proudly *A Mighty Fortress* every Reformation Sunday (we were all in the choir except for Mom who was the organist), and it literally gave me goose bumps!

---

[164] Armstrong, *Spiral Staircase*, 272.

[165] Armstrong, *Spiral Staircase*, 272.

[166] Armstrong, *Spiral Staircase*, 297.

[167] Armstrong, *Spiral Staircase*, 298.

While much of Lutheranism is basic 16th century Christianity, rife with the fallen nature of humankind and our inescapable sinfulness, Luther added a unique concept in the mix, which he named *Anfechtung*. Though there is no exact English equivalent term, Anfechtung has been translated alternately as temptation or trial, the latter being the preferred choice of my pastor. We were taught in our confirmation class that God tested us, gave us trials meant to "drive us to Jesus' feet seeking forgiveness." As if that were not enough, Anfechtungen (the plural form of Anfechtung) were also the primary tools of Satan. In short, we humans were hopeless because we would never be able to tell if it was God or Satan who was assailing us with the Anfectungen. The best we would ever hope for was God's grace, and even that we could not earn – it was just given out of God's infinite mercy.

In Luther's *Large Catechism*, he spends a bit more time describing Anfectungen and adds – in a way that seems to place himself in a different class – that those who are occupied with spiritual matters are plagued even more by these trials (much in the way Campbell later described).[168] It was a concept that intrigued me because even at that age, I knew deeply that I had a strong relationship with God. And it was not too many years later that, as a senior in high school, I heard my call to the ministry. I had not yet read of Luther's dark night of the soul nor had I ever heard of such a thing.

My first experience was simply a falling out, of sorts. Like the young Mother Teresa, I was in love – at least that is how I would describe the feeling I had about God. But that innocent crush was not prepared for the tests of a first year seminarian's questions, and certainly was not rigorous enough to withstand the slicing and dicing of theological studies (as Weems so accurately describes). Eventually my skipping across campus from Colby Chapel to classes became more of a death march and the crush faded into dusty memory. It is hard to place a finger on exactly when and how, but by the end of my second semester at ANTS, at the ripe age of 22, I left my dreams of ordination behind and returned to studying psychology.

Though my relationship with God was repaired over the next few years, there were other dips and setbacks, some more spiritual resulting from my questioning my former call, and some resulting from life crashes – like a too-early divorce from my first love after only three years of marriage. Because of my faith tradition and spiritual practices at the time, I turned to prayer – my times of "conversation" with God. But despite my sincerity that quickly disintegrated into what I called "versations" – there was no "con" to it; no God,

---

[168] To check the validity of my recollections I reviewed a seminal article on Luther's concepts: "The Concept of *Anfechtungen* in Luther's Thought," by David P. Scaer, in *Concordia Theological Quarterly* 47, no.1, (January 1983): 15-30.

just me talking, and asking, and then begging, but nothing happened. At first I though that these were my trials – my Anfechtungen – and that if I could pass the test, my faith would be restored. But it lasted for a year, almost, until at a retreat at a Franciscan friary. I had been meditating alone in the chapel at night, focused on the crucifix, when suddenly I heard the hammer strike the nail in his hand. And, just like that, the feeling – and the voice – was there again. Only this time the feeling was different; deeper in my guts, haunting, and even a bit scary. I was so taken, so relieved, that I just began sobbing uncontrollably. I thought, "You're back," and just as quickly got the understanding that it had never left me – it was I who had become lost. Ebb and flow – "It's like breathing," one of the monks had said, "just breathe with it." So it went like that for several years, coming and fading, like Weems' seasons, and with it slight changes each time in the feeling and relatedness I had with the God of my understanding. But the bottom line of this time is that I was clear that I did not want to be called by God. I had given up on my calling. I began acting out, trying to prove God was wrong, that God had the wrong guy and was totally mistaken. I felt unholy and unworthy. I stopped talking to God, though I really do not know when. It just wasn't part of my routine anymore.

But nothing prepared me for the "dark time" as I call it. It was a several year period of estrangement from anything holy. Brought on by a second divorce and the recognition that I had precipitated that hellishness in the relationship, I fell into despair, not just socially (at one point I could count all of my friends on one hand, two of which were my children), but especially spiritually. I felt diseased, not just bad or unworthy – I was broken and irreparable. Somewhere in the darkness of that time I began reading again. But even that was of no comfort. One day I picked up my Bible and let it fall open (having always believed that whatever one read in the Bible it would have meaning and applicability to one's current situation). But it fell open to Judges 19 somewhere in the middle of a description of an outsider traveling through a foreign land where the townsmen brutally raped his female companion and left her to die on the doorstep. I threw the Bible across the room and cursed. What did that have to do with anything spiritual? I was totally lost in my spirituality. And I felt entirely alone and abandoned in life. Maybe it was I who had been left naked to die on the doorstep!

Nowadays, over three decades later, I still cannot place dates, street addresses or beginnings and endings to relationships from that time. Though I am required each year, as an owner of a preschool, to file a CORI report that goès as far back as 1975, I still struggle trying to fill in the dates between 1984 and 1989 – the time sequence is folded and twisted, the leases and addresses just don't add up. It was like I had been in some kind of vortex of time and space that scrambled it all. It was, for me, the darkest night of my soul.

Since that time I have had many more trips to and through the dark night. Much like my old Franciscan mentor advised me, it had become more like breathing, and far less like times of good and bad. Through the nights, I have lost all distinctions of good and bad. It just is – things and events just are – a part of living and believing. I suppose from time to time I wish I could be one of those believers whose faith is so rock solid that it never seems to fluctuate, but that is not my experience. In the final chapter I will speak more about where my beliefs lie today.

Summary
Through these four stories we can see several emerging themes that will be explored in the following chapters.

- Each of the writers described her experience in terms of sadness and at times depression. Mother Teresa described her sadness in almost the way a spurned lover speaks of her beloved. Her constant prayer was to give herself over completely to her groom and the pain she felt in not hearing even a word of support from this Jesus she loved so dearly was devastating. Renita Weems, on the other hand mourned the loss of that starry-eyed innocence that she had at the revival tents and that she saw in young college students she now mentored. The sadness she felt at knowing that had to die for that student mixed with her own nostalgia for the feelings of zeal made it doubly hard for her. Karen Armstrong's sadness was more like a grief over a lost life spent in the darkness of misdiagnosed disease – though she never wondered if she would have held onto her simplistic belief had events been otherwise. And like those three, I certainly recall feelings of loss and sadness in my periods of the dark night.
- Each, though discouraged and feeling a sense that it was fruitless, all continued with their spiritual practice of prayer or meditation. For me, my experience with scripture reading as a form of lectio divina became absurd in one moment reading a violent passage in Judges, but even in my cursing prayer, I was still praying. Teresa of Calcutta prayed continually each day, without ceasing, despite hearing and feeling nothing for all those years. Weems described her temptation to walk away and Armstrong kept trying out prayer

and meditation almost even when she no longer believed as a test to see if any feeling returned.

- Clearly the precipitator of each of the described dark nights was different, and those differences colored the nature and flavor of the dark nights that were described. But what was similar was the slow realization of the onset of the darkness or absence of God. As it increased, Mother Teresa wrote, "Pray for me. The longing for God is so terribly painful, and yet the darkness is becoming greater."[169] Weems' description of the changing seasons gives the impression of the slow unfolding of the process, and that there was no way to rush the seasons. And by contrast, Karen Armstrong's darkness was so convoluted by her epilepsy that identifying when her spiritual dryness and darkness actually began is difficult to pinpoint. Others, like me, may experience the dark night in multiple phases, each with its own different precipitating event.

- However what was most revealing was that each person came away from the experience with a deeper and more profound connection with God. And perhaps more importantly, each developed a sense of compassion for others' spiritual journey. Mother Teresa's compassion was evident in her work, "Today God loves the world so much that He gives you, He gives me, to love the world, to be His love, His compassion." And speaking of the poor and dying, she added, "Tuberculosis and cancer are not the great diseases. I think the greater disease is to be unwanted, unloved."[170] Renita Weems characterized the result of the dark night as leaving us "with a painful, exquisite insight into what it means to be human before a loving God."[171] But Karen Armstrong's testament to the dark night comes not so much in her autobiographical texts, but in her opus magnum, *The Great Transformation*. In that text she points to the evidence that every one of the Axial sages reached the same conclusion that the dark night of a people's soul, of a civilization's soul, is the teaching of compassion. "Past distress brings us back to the Golden Rule; it should help us see that other people's suffering is as important as

---

[169] Kolodiejchuk, *Mother Teresa*, 174.

[170] Kolodiejchuk, *Mother Teresa*, 206.

[171] Weems, *Listening*, 174.

our own – even (perhaps especially) the anguish of our enemies. Compassion and concern for everybody was the best policy [as determined by the sages]. We should take their advice seriously because they were the experts."[172] For me the finale was to return to theology school and study my faith more deeply. Somehow we all return home.

In the following chapters we will examine more closely what changes and how those changes take place. Were they inherent in the basic theology of the individuals going through the experience or are those changes the results of the work within the dark night of the soul?

---

[172] Karen Armstrong, *The Great Transformation.* (New York: Alfred Knopf, 2006), 396-7.

Chapter Four – Spiritual Wounds:
Gathering Data from Travelers in the Dark

*Yes, there were nights of great loss. Yes, the soul suffered from
fearful subtractions. Yes, a great emptiness opened up where I had
stored my spiritual treasures, and yet. And yet what? And yet what
remained when everything else was gone was more real than
anything I could have imagined. I was no longer apart from what I
sought; I was part of it, or in it. I'm sorry I can't say it any better
than that. There was no place else I wanted to be.* [173]

Barbara Brown Taylor

The question that arises from reading personal accounts is whether these
individual stories are typical of dark night experiences or just individual
anomalies. Are there commonalities across multiple people and if so what do
those common themes suggest? To answer these questions, I designed a simple
questionnaire that could be used with a small population of clerics. As stated in
the first chapter, I chose to focus on persons in the ordained ministry because I
held the hypothesis that the "crisis" presented by the dark night of the soul, that is,
an apparent loss of connectivity with the Divine, was or could be more
threatening, more impactful to a minister, whose very vocation lay in the realm of
spirituality, than it may be for an average, church-going individual.

The questionnaire was a fifteen-item survey that blended multiple-choice,
forced-choice and narrative-answer type of questions. Respondents completed the
survey anonymously. The questionnaire was approved by the Faculty
Subcommittee on Human Subjects Research at Andover Newton Theological
School. The full survey is attached in Appendix A.

Participants in the study were ordained ministers in two protestant
denominations: Lutherans (specifically, ministers in the Evangelical Lutheran
Church of America, ELCA, New England Synod) and Methodists (specifically,
ministers in the United Methodist Church, UMC, New England Synod). These
two populations were accessible to me through my own personal connections and
are not assumed to be either representative populations of ministers in general nor
of ministers within their respective denominations. Access to the Lutheran
ministers was gained with the support of the Reverend Jim Hazelwood, Bishop of
the ELCA New England Synod. Access to the Methodist ministers was gained
through my daughter, Reverend Rebecca Girrell, then minister of Trinity UMC,
Montpelier, Vermont during her participation in the annual UMC regional
conference. Response to the questionnaire was voluntary self-selection.

---

[173] Barbara Brown Taylor, *Learning to Walk in the Dark* (New York: HarperOne, 2014),
146.

Before beginning, let me caution readers that these data should not be viewed as statistically valid observations. The survey questions were not normed on any population for construct validity and the sampling technique, as was described, was simply done by engaging circles of my associates – so it should in no way be seen as representative of population data. The sole purpose of the survey used in this study was to gather anecdotal information from a larger population of today's ministers and to see how they articulate their experiences of the dark night and its effect on the progression of their spiritual evolution.

However with those cautions considered, the results of this simple survey do show some interesting common threads. There seems to be a consistency between these two denominations with regard to the dark night experience and with respect to its nature, duration, and overall impact on personal theology and belief systems.

Demographics of the survey

Ninety-one members of the clergy responded, somewhat evenly divided between male (48) and female (42) (one did not identify gender) whose years in ministry ranged from only 3 years to 56 (with an average tenure of 21.35 years in service). Denominationally I had 49 Lutherans (ELCA), 26 Methodists (UMC), 9 Jews and a few individuals in other denominations (UU, UCC Episcopalian and Catholic). Most were married (59), ten were single, five divorced, 4 in committed gay/lesbian relationships and a scattering of other comments not fitting those categories. The rabbis surveyed were asked to participate out of my curiosity and as a result of conversations with Jewish friends who insisted that either Jews never felt a dark night experience or said that every day is a rising out of a dark night – their contention being that, in fact, Judaism was a religion steeped in the dark nights of captivity, slavery and oppression such that Judaism did not consider the dark night to be a phenomenon apart or separate from everyday life. Though fairly similar in their collective responses, the nine rabbis were not factored into the following discussion.

The first question on the survey asked how often participants had experienced what they would identify as a dark night experience and 11 of the Christian respondents disqualified themselves as having never had such an experience. Thus the observations following are based on the remaining 71 Christian respondents who self identified as having had at least one dark night experience.[174]

---

[174] One rabbi was in this original grouping and thus was not counted in the final analysis of the Christian respondents.

Only one of the demographic categories had any substantial differentiating characteristic: Gender was a factor only on precipitating event where several females identified childbirth, miscarriage and sexual assault as precipitating events of the dark night experience as opposed to none (obviously) of the males identifying any such issues. However beyond the precipitators, there were no apparent gender differences excepting for a slightly younger mean age of female ministers than their male counterparts as the chart below shows.

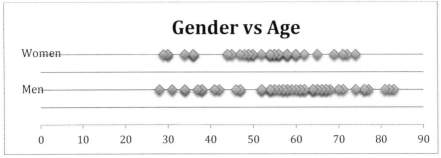

Figure 2. Gender vs Age Demographics

The two main groups in the survey (Lutherans and Methodists) showed no noticeable difference in how they responded to the questions. And finally age was not a predictor of the number of dark night experiences, as seen in Figure 3 below.

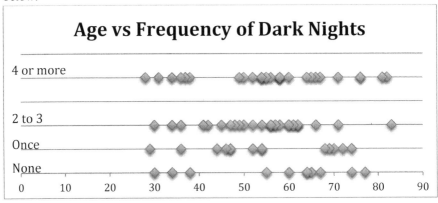

Figure 3. Age vs. Frequency of Dark Night Experiences

Narrative

As previously noted, I took on the topic of the dark night of the soul because my personal spiritual journey was mostly characterized by periods of spiritual dryness punctuated by occasional touches of blissful connection. Yet throughout all of these times I found very little literature to support my experience and fewer ministers who would engage with me in the dialogue about it. However as a result of this brief survey, I now find that my experience is not at all uncommon but rather may be the norm with only a little more than ten percent of those I surveyed saying that they had *not* experienced some form of the dark night.

The dark night of the soul is loosely defined for the respondents of the survey as any period of dryness in one's connectedness with God or relationship with the Divine which can last anywhere from a few days to well over a year. Most respondents (69.5%) had multiple dark night experiences (three or more) but reported that it varied widely in length (30% saying it was totally unpredictable, 27% saying it lasted a few months to a year and 20% stating that the "night" lasted more than a year). The variance in length may be a result of the nature of the precipitating event or the nature of the belief being acted upon during the dark night but the design of the survey did not permit investigating those variables.

How often have you experienced what you might consider a dark night of the soul?

Answered: 83   Skipped: 0

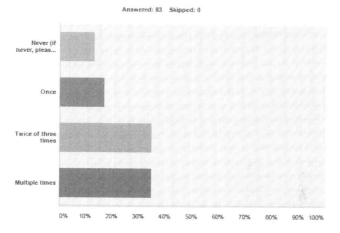

For ministers in this survey, the dark night experience seems to be most frequently precipitated by innocent suffering – either on the part of the believer or the suffering of those perceived to be innocent and undeserving of that suffering (situations like 9/11 and Newtown, Connecticut being typical examples listed by 53% of the respondents). When the tragedy strikes close to home, there is an accompanying feeling of abandonment by God (a sense of broken heart – or it all gets too heavy, checked by 54.6%), which is particularly difficult for those in the ministry.

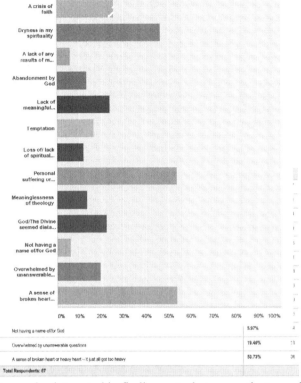

How would you generally describe experience that marked the onset of your dark night(s)? (check all that apply)

Answered: 67   Skipped: 16

I was also interested in finding out what respondents used as their main form of spiritual practice and if that was where the disruption of the dark night occurred. And indeed 46% of the Christian respondents listed some form of prayer as their primary spiritual practice with another 17.9% listing meditation (walking or sitting) as their primary form. Yet most chose continued prayer and meditation as the resource or practice they held onto to get them through the dark night (58.8%) with a significant personal relationship falling in at a close second (57.3%). Interestingly, other clergy or clergy group was a means for coping with the dark night employed by 50% of the respondents.

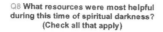

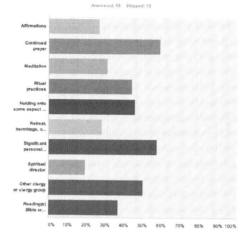

One of the dark soul with more frightening aspects of the night of the is wrestling one's personal demons. Question 9 of the survey asked: "Were there any particular issues that seemed more difficult or painful to deal with during the experience of your dark night(s)?" Topics that were listed as the most difficult challenges during the dark night were widely varied but clustered in a few areas. (This question was an open response item)

- The first major grouping of difficult issues was the job/role of being in ministry while experiencing the dark night of the soul. Sermons and services felt dry and perfunctory; several reported feeling abandoned or rejected by their religious community or by synod leadership; trying to make enough sense of the faith journey to preach each week; a loss of trust in the pastoral office; and the double bind of having felt called by a God who no longer sustains one in that call.

- Personal events and personal life issues – things like loneliness, loss of job or removal from my office, were listed along with "living" in general, feeling selfish and questioning my calling was a second fairly large group.

- A third theme that emerged was more psychological in nature. People questioned their sanity, or worthiness, and feelings of hopelessness. Others experienced anxiety attacks or panic, loss of sleep and feelings of betrayal or forsakenness.
- The fourth cluster centered around theological questions: doubts that God made sense or even existed, theodicy, the trinity, and aspects of main-line systematics, (e.g., the meaning and understanding of Grace as Lutherans hold it), and a feeling of being trapped in a system of belief that no longer fit who they were as a believer.
- There were many more mostly personal themes – that were heartbreaking in the raw honesty with which the respondents spoke of their struggles and grieving.

I also asked (in an open response question) what other resources and readings were helpful during the passage through the dark night, and got a short list of books and references (many of which were not even Christian in nature).

- Authors like Samuel Powel, Shakti Gawain and Joan Borysenko; Standard classics like Kubler-Ross, Jackson, Granger, Bonhoeffer, King (Jr), and Stringfellow
- Mystical writers from multiple faith traditions, from Jewish mystics, the Sufists, and Buddhists to contemporary poets like Mary Oliver and David Whyte. Some even listed the Bhagavad Gita and the Tao Te Ching
- Books like *Holy the Firm, Listening for God, Good Grief, When the Heart Waits* and of course the Bible and the Psalms in particular were among the readings listed as helpful.
- And frequently mentioned, though no specific titles were listed, was the use of music and dance.

Eventually the dark night lifts and the light reappears. For most people (56.1%) in the survey this was a slow and gradual dawn as opposed to waking up one day with it gone (7%). Nearly 20% felt that the end of the dark night experience felt more like being touched by the Divine. There was a sense of purging and relief that was far beyond the normal realm. However I think that the most profound single result of the survey was that over 75% of the respondents of all religious traditions stated that their faith had been strengthened by the dark night experience, with another 20% saying that their faith remained unchanged and was what they held onto during the dark night.

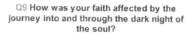

Q9 How was your faith affected by the journey into and through the dark night of the soul?

Answered: 62 Skipped: 21

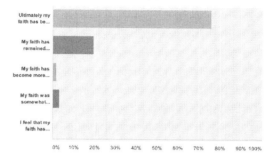

Answer Choices		Responses	
Ultimately my faith has been strengthened by the experience		75.81%	47
My faith has remained unchanged - I always held onto faith or the belief that God was there (somewhere) just out of my reach		19.35%	12
My faith has become more fragile (something I must care for) as a result		1.61%	1
My faith was somewhat altered or somehow lessened		3.23%	2
I feel that my faith has slipped significantly as a result		0.00%	0
Total			62

Analysis

The dark night of the soul is a sintering crucible – a place of purification – where previously functional but unchallenged beliefs and attitudes are burned away. One respondent stated that after his/her dark night experience "I was less arrogant about my beliefs," and another added, "I became more gentle with others who were struggling." The dark night is in one person's words "a call to a deep healing and personal transformation," where one comes to "a more honest appraisal of my brokenness," as another commented. Faith emerges as a gift instead of a right and with each foray into the dark night the individual becomes clearer that those experiences of God, which we assume are God in full, "are not God, but just glimpses" and foretastes of the fullness of God.

Interestingly, many responding to the survey discussed their grief – which came in many forms. There was grieving for the loss of a simpler belief structure that was all neat and clean. Some spoke of the grief they had to feel when the God of their understanding no longer served to whitewash their pain away, while others simply spoke of the pain of living and experiencing life as it is. But in all of these instances, learning to incorporate one's own personal grief and validating others' grief was a common theme that spanned the entire survey population. Several spoke of seeking other non-Christian sources to help them cope with their pain and grief.

Another common thread among the comments is that each trip back into the dark night becomes less scary and less foreboding. Respondents seem to understand that it is a necessary part of the journey and that one comes to understand God better the more one strips away what one thought or knew. Respondents became comfortable with the "anxious moments" and came to trust that the anxiety is the feeling of "falling into God through trust" as one characterized it. One person wrote that as a result of several deeply painful dark night experiences, "I am more solid, less arrogant, more compassionate and less certain." The same person went on to add that s/he was, however, far "less tolerant of the endless squabbles in church and denominational life." They just didn't matter as much anymore.

While prayer and meditation were the most frequently employed spiritual practices and the places where the darkness and dryness were most perceptible, what most participants came away with is a deepened commitment to regular, daily prayer and meditation. This is not so much ritual prayer and liturgical prayer but personal or private time seeking and listening for God. "I now pray no matter how I feel," one said. "I cling tighter to God now and when I can't feel God's presence I beg him to hold on to me."

However not all of the open responses focused on prayer. Many stressed the importance of self-care and being gentle with one's self, respecting and insisting on boundaries, and ensuring sabbatical, journaling and reflection time. Persistence in any of the spiritual disciplines was a cornerstone for many, while others sought alternate communities of support (a hermitage, for one, a retreat center, or a group of peer pastors for others). And more than one respondent found liberation through learning how to scream and curse at God (in the full Joban tradition of our forbearers). "My practice became freer, less ritualistic and structured. God keeps inviting me to experience more of him, relying less on the ritual without abandoning the spiritual practices and basics."

On the theological level, I asked respondents if they could articulate how, if at all, their perception of God had changed. For about a half dozen respondents, their perception of God was unaltered. But for the rest, removing their blinders and previous conceptions of God allowed them to see God in many more wonderful, beautiful and compassionate ways.

Though God became much less "picture-able" as one put it, God was far more present in everything, "more transcendent and more immanent." Mostly these comments came as a result of seeing God as more personally present. "Instead of looking for God out there, I trust God is within me and I need to be still to be connected." "God is always there/here – I just need to center down to experience that." "I am trying to learn what it means to live by grace and with grace and in grace. I am working on understanding God in a more informal sense rather than as a cold, distant, and unapproachable father."

Many comments echoed the mystics' claim that their "inner most being is God" as the mystics said. "I no longer look for God out there. I have a new understanding of incarnation. We were given Jesus so that we could understand that God was not 'out there' but alive and living through and in us." God has become more intimate. The experience left one with the feeling that "we have been through the trenches together. God has seen me at my most despondent. I now watch more closely for the Holy Spirit around me – and it continually surprises me!"

There were so many more personal statements that speak to a growing intimacy and understanding – yet an understanding that is based in mystery and not knowing. But this one summed up the dark night as best as any of them: "Out of love God shakes the foundations of any and all idols we create of him; the dark night opens us up to truer experiences of God as God is, not as we imagine him to be."

Having had such experiences, travelers on the inward journey of faith gained some valuable insights they use for themselves and would willingly share with others. Some are as simple as "knowing that there is always more to come, I fear it less," and "I now know I can endure through the experience because God has never left me." "Now I know to wait patiently – though there are no guarantees." Several even characterized this as a "Footsteps" experience. But one person said rather matter-of-factly, "In theory, it prepares you; in actuality dark nights are dark nights and one must walk through them." And maybe this says it too: "I am less fearful – but still alert."

I would be remiss not to include two direct quotes that eloquently speak to the full meaning of the dark night of the soul.

- "I'm beginning to wonder if the idea of the "dark night" is more common, and might even be the norm for some people, who can't embrace the dominant American religion of optimism. Perhaps my problem is trying to "fix" my dark night, and instead accept that it is another path into the reality of God. "

- "I don't know. I think I'm more equipped for ministry because it is all so very real for me, now. I am more sensitive to people who feel far away from God. I preach about this, how, finally, God said, you know what? Your emotions are important. I created them. But they're not so powerful as to negate my existence or send/push me away. When I heard that inside, I thought, oh, yeah! My emotions AREN'T that powerful! How silly of me to have thought so. God IS here. God HAS BEEN here. God WILL BE here. I might not FEEL HIM NEAR. But it doesn't mean he ISN'T. Seems simple, in hindsight. But truly a piece of wisdom I wouldn't have received if I hadn't gone through the experience."

Lastly, respondents were asked if they would write a short description of their dark night experiences, and some shared. What they shared – though mostly the facts and events of their life experiences and precipitating events – was crushing and humbling. These are the real stories of the dark night, which, shared in confidence are full of revealing personal information. Some of them caused me to weep, some made me wince in pain. But none left me untouched. Stories of sexual assault and rape, stories of divorce and lost relationships and stories of absolute and utter desolation spoke volumes about how vulnerable and fragile one's faith can be. The soul – the meaning-maker that rests in the greater being of God – searches in desperation for some meaningful interpretation when none could be or would be found. Questions of theodicy don't hold water within the greater understanding of God as love. Reading stories of others' dark nights swelled my heart with compassion. If we do not learn how better to listen to those brothers and sisters among us who deal with this process, we run the risk of being the church/community that – as so many reported was the case – abandoned them and hung them out to dry at the most critical point in their faith journey.

Perhaps our Jewish brothers and sisters have done it right – every Shabbat service contains a time for mourning; every Shabbat service includes psalms of pain and suffering; and their liturgical year sanctifies and ritualized the history of dark nights, exile, and slavery. One rabbi wrote, "I grew up with doubt and anger at God as a fundamental element of my Jewish identity along side faith and commitment; not an either/or." Another told me (in dialogue after calling for clarification about the introduction to the survey), "Job is perhaps the least example of what you might call dark night experiences. Look at every story – Moses, Abraham, Isaac, Jacob, David – all of them and all of the stories, lived with and through pain and suffering and the sense of absence and presence of their Lord. It is who we are." Perhaps she is more right than she knows – perhaps it is who we all are.

Listening to these stories and reading the comments of ministers who have walked through the dark night of the soul one must conclude that the dark night of the soul is neither a singular nor an uncommon experience. It may be in fact an integral element of the inward journey of faith. For those in the ministry who see their path as actively living what they preach and dole out in their ministering to others, it may well be a natural by-product of the work. The problem one faces in reading these accounts is that, while in retrospect, those who have endured the dark night can make some sense of it, during the process we are mostly unable to name what is happening spiritually, psychologically or theologically. What is clear and unquestionable is that the net effect of the dark night experience most often strengthens one's faith in and relationship with the Divine.

Pulling Together the Threads

Saint John of the Cross explored and mapped out the territory of the dark night of the soul using the descriptors of his day. Through his writings and explanations of his mystical poetry, we get a glimpse of what transpires through the dark night, of how God works silently within us and how our ego-driven understanding is affected, if not destroyed, in order to make way for the direct experience of God's love. It is my contention though that, despite his labeling of the night of the spirit and then night of the senses, despite breaking the process into active and passive nights, what John of the Cross was describing is a holistic process; one that is taking place on a number of differing levels often concurrently. His language seems to suggest a linear or stepwise process, but may in fact just be a number of different attempts of describing the ways in which this process happens. However in personally describing their experiences of the dark night, neither the abstracted authors (Mother Teresa, Renita Weems or Karen Armstrong) nor the respondents to the clergy survey sliced up their descriptions either the same way as John of the Cross did or even as any other person seemed to have described it. This however does not refute the sainted mystic's nomenclature nor invalidate these modern day persons' experience. It simply points to the fact that under the more clinical scrutiny of the mystic's microscope more may be discernable than meets the naked "eye" of the common writer of today.

Both John of the Cross and his English predecessor and author of *The Cloud of Unknowing* cite contemplation as the driver of the process with ample warnings about not applying this outside the world of the most serious spiritual seeker. And despite John's solitary confinement and whippings, neither he nor *The Cloud* talk about the precipitating events that seem to be part of the cited authors' and respondents' understanding of the onset of the dark night. Irrespective of this obvious difference, however, the similarities between the modern class of dark night experiences and those described by John of the Cross seem elsewhere to be in sync.

John of the Cross described both how one's desire for one's old, tried-and-true spiritual practices wanes, and how the feeling they provide simply dries up. In a similar fashion we see examples of how Weems no longer could tolerate her old ways, or how prayer became empty for Armstrong and how both were so painfully evident to Mother Teresa. Respondents to the clergy survey likewise pointed to the loss of vitality in their prayer life and of dropping their old ways. Perhaps the distinction Gerald May makes is more helpful to point out and may explain some of the descriptive differences. May wrote, that the dark night is "the ongoing spiritual process of our lives. We have periodic conscious awareness of it, but it continues at all times, hidden within us. We are aware only of the experiences that come to our consciousness. Thus what someone might call 'going through the dark night' I would call 'having an experience of the dark night.'"[175]

So these experiences come and go (according to our awareness) as described by the sampled population. But three things remain common across all populations – including John of the Cross, Teresa of Avila and *The Cloud's* author: the seeker of unitive love in God becomes freer, less encumbered by life's trivialities and attachments; spiritual practices like prayer and meditation shift from conceptual, word-based exchanges to contemplative resting in God and an openness to whatever comes of that; and there is an awakening to the already/always connection with and in God. It is the realization of "our essential union with God and all creation."[176]

In all of these it would appear that the modern day cohort is speaking of exactly the same experience and transformation as John of the Cross despite using a different vocabulary, different descriptors and having different precipitators.

In the following chapter I will hypothesize what is happening in this transformative shift and propose a method for understanding the changes in language and attitudes of the believer traveling through the dark nights of the soul.

---

[175] May, *Dark Night*, 186-7.

[176] May, *Dark Night*, 184.

Chapter Five – Walking With A Limp
The Transformative Effect

Jacob was left alone; and a man wrestled with him until daybreak. When the man saw that he did not prevail against Jacob, he struck him on the hip socket and Jacob's hip was put out of joint as he wrestled with him.
Genesis 32:21-25 (New Oxford Annotated Bible)

> *While a crisis is a summons into transformation, we must also*
> *recognize that it's an advent into entanglement of feelings. Part of*
> *living a crisis creatively is identifying and understanding the feelings*
> *that come with it. Otherwise, we don't have a crisis; it has us.* [177]
>
> Sue Monk Kidd

How do we identify and name what is happening during the dark night of the soul? What is the action and effect of the dark night? And perhaps most importantly, what are the implications for practice to which these data point? In this chapter, I want to outline what I believe are the actions and net effects of the dark night experience (both perceived as well as the unseen and on-going aspects) and how one might proceed based in this understanding. My intent of this chapter is threefold:

- To weave together the insights and common threads recognized in the previous chapters into a cohesive landscape showing some of the changes that result from the dark night of the soul,
- To compare those insights with the prevailing theories of spiritual development schemas and perhaps expose some gaps in the current thought regarding spiritual development, and
- To propose a comprehensive and systematic way of viewing the language, thoughts and issues confronted by spiritual persons as they travel in and out of the dark night of the soul.

In doing so I hope to provide practitioners in the field of ministry – both ministers and those who may minister to them – with a better way of understanding where such persons are in their spiritual journey so that we might be of better support and service to them on their journey. It has been my contention throughout this thesis that because so little is known of what transpires during the dark nights and how that affects one's language and thought processes, most of those who pass this way feel under-supported at best and misunderstood at worst.

It would appear from the previous three chapters that the dark night of the soul evolves or transforms the believer and results in not only a new way of being but in a new way of seeing. Paul may be writing of this transformation when he described his new way of seeing to the Corinthians. "When I was a child, I spoke like a child, I thought like a child, I reasoned like a child; when I became an adult, I put an end to childish ways. For now we see in a mirror, dimly, but then we will

[177] Sue Monk Kidd, *When the Heart Waits: Spiritual Direction for Life's Sacred Questions* (New York: HarperCollins, 1990), 93.

see face to face." John of the Cross, in a very uncharacteristic chapter of *The Dark Night* describes the process as a ten-step "ladder of love" in *The Dark Night of the Soul* that describes how the soul is affected at each phase in the quest for unity.[178] However these rungs on the ladder are not particularly prescriptive and even somewhat nebulously descriptive. He says the steps are: The languishing of the soul; seeking God without ceasing; having the fervor so as not to fail; habituated suffering without weariness; longing for God impatiently; running in hope toward God to touch Him repeatedly; becoming vehement in boldness; seizing God and holding fast to God; burning with sweetness; and becoming wholly assimilated into God. While these steps may in some way identify an active participation in the dark night experience, one is still left with a question of how one describes the depth and breadth of the experience along the way. Not surprisingly, modern psychologists and spiritual directors use similar hierarchical and linear language in describing stages of spiritual development.

If modern science has taught us anything it is that the human species is a result of a continual evolution, inextricably woven together with the evolution of our planet and of the ever-evolving universe. Julian Huxley is purported to have written, "We are nothing more than evolution becoming conscious of itself." That being the case, it is only logical to assume that our spirituality should be an evolving and dynamic aspect of that consciousness. But how do we transform in this process of faith? If Paul is not simply talking about some eschatological state but rather about the evolution of one's understanding, then how does that shift in understanding happen? For the greater part of the church history and for the majority of the post-enlightenment theologians, that movement was seen as a path of ascent, a ladder as described above, a stairway to heaven. Through the disciplines of prayer and contemplation the seeker was taught how to purify thought and master the self. As self-mastery was attained the energy of the seeker became strong enough (most often described as a higher state) to maintain contact with the higher reaches of consciousness until one converges on that unitive point where oneness with the Divine is achieved. But this may not be the only path, and certainly not the path of the dark night. Cynthia Bourgeault writes,

> There is another route to center: a more reckless path and extravagant path, which is attained not through storing up that energy or concentrating the life force, but through throwing it all away – or giving it all away. The unitive point is reached not through concentration of being but through the free squandering of it; not through acquisition or attainment but through self-emptying; not through "up" but through "down." This is the way of

---

[178] John of the Cross, *Dark Night*, 92-98. The steps on the ladder don't lend themselves to the discussion at hand but are mentioned as a point of reference.

kenosis, the revolutionary path that Jesus introduced into the consciousness of the West.[179]

And it is the way of the mystics like John of the Cross (the greater portion of the writings of John of the Cross describe a kenotic process). The exercises and processes of the dark night passage were described more as this type of self-emptying than the mainline church's ladder-like and staircase processes. Mother Teresa wrote, "Even God could do nothing for someone already full. You have to be completely empty to let Him in to do what He will. That's the most beautiful part of God, eh? Being almighty, and yet not forcing Himself on anyone."[180] And while Armstrong described her return to unitive spirituality as "the spiral staircase," she was referring more to the feeling of coming up from a deep hole, a "climb out of darkness," rather than an ascent into heaven.

How, then, is that self-emptying process to be understood? What shifted inside each of the believers whose voices filled the last two chapters? If the dark night of the soul is just an occasional experience for a few, one might make certain assertions about this anomaly. But as we have seen, the bulk of the ministers surveyed experienced what they consider a dark night of the soul and most experienced it not once but multiple times. Thus it might be that for those for whom their faith life is an integral part of their self concept, the dark night of the soul may be more like a human psychological experience. If that is the case, it could be helpful to borrow some language from the field of human psychology and the nature of the cognitive/moral development, however, doing so runs the risk of overlaying the observations with the hypotheses of previous researchers – and it is precisely those assumptions of linearity and irreversibility with which I take exception.[181] My assertion and my exception to the bulk of this research follows Loder's contention when he writes, "The human sciences are the human spirit attempting to understand itself, but by itself it is a loose cannon of creativity, accordingly, the human sciences are a baseless search for the

---

[179] Cynthia Bourgeault, *The Wisdom Jesus, Transforming Heart and Mind – a New Perspective on Christ and His Message* (Boston: Shambala, 2008), 66.

[180] Kolodiejchuk, *Mother Theresa,* 260.

[181] The field of developmental psychology, as characterized by Erikson, Piaget, Vygotsky and Bronfenbrenner, as well as theories of moral development such as those proposed by Kohlberg, Perry and Gilligan have long held that the key drivers of development (cognitive, moral and spiritual) are simply the aging process and the increasing complexity of the challenges and responsibilities faced at different ages. The majority of these theories purport that the greatest advancements are through the ages of childhood and adolescence and that development relatively levels off once one reaches adulthood. Fowler's stage theory follows the Eriksonian pattern and translates Erikson's cognitive and psychosocial development into the language of faith.

ground of the human spirit. This search is doomed to repeat in its outcomes the same essential shortcomings and limitations that drove the human spirit to begin the search."[182]

As I described in the introductory chapter, my theoretical understanding of the self is based on a mixture of the Jungian notions of the little self (mind/ego) and the big SELF (soul/spirit), mixed with developmental theories of Erikson (as portrayed by Loder and Fowler) and a healthy dose of constructivist theory. What this leads to is a sense that there is a learned and practiced way of seeing oneself that evolves with maturity based on experiences and their interaction with the stored (and ever growing/changing/developing) perception of self. This circular, self-referring loop of logic either confirms or refutes the previously held self-concept and results in a more firmly held belief or exposes it as erroneous and in need of modification.

Ultimately the process of developing a self-concept and a sense of self-esteem produces a systematic understanding of the world and one's place within it. As matured or maturing adults we arrive at a place wherein our minds (read that as our little self or egoic self) have constructed a system of understanding, a systematic philosophy, that "makes sense" out of the rather chaotic world around us. It is this system of logic that James Fowler sees evolving in his classic text, *Stages of Faith* and to which James Loder refers in *The Logic of the Spirit* that I wish to explore and expand based on what we have observed in the discussions of the first four chapters.

Based on his and others' research[183] and his observations as a psychotherapist, Fowler proposes a system of stages that describe the evolution of the spiritual journey from childhood through adulthood.[184] However, the greater portion of Fowler's stage theory deals with the evolution of logic through childhood and teen years, and most adults, he says, do not reach stage five until midlife, after which he finds very little evidence of persons making it much further in their spiritual development. Our survey population and the selected authors we have reviewed are all in their mid-life and beyond. And it would appear from reading their responses or reflections that a great deal more is happening and can happen within their spiritual lives. The concept of God does not remain static and fixed but evolves along with the belief/unbelief that the spiritual seeker experiences.

---

[182] Loder, *Logic of the Spirit*, 39.

[183] Fowler's model is based on his own original research with over 300 subjects, combined with the research of Eugene Mischey (University of Toronto) and Richard Shulik (University of Chicago) and are detailed in the appendix of *Stages of Faith*.

[184] Because some of the language of Fowler's stage theory is included within the model I will propose, a brief chart summarizing his stages is included in Appendix B.

Contrary to Fowler's stages, I would like to introduce the concept of "operating states[185]" (much like the operating systems of a computer) more because the language is more temporal and fluid characteristic than that of stages. Ken Wilbur makes a great distinction between states and stages. Essentially he says that stages are developed levels of abilities gained through repeated practice, much like the mastery of a skill might be. States on the other hand are transitory and can be visited or experienced despite functioning at a "lower" stage of development. "With repeated practice of contacting higher states, your own stages of development will tend to unfold in a much faster and easier way. There is, in fact, considerable experimental evidence demonstrating exactly that. The more you are plunged into authentic higher states of consciousness, the faster you will grow and develop through any of the stages of consciousness."[186] I have adopted Wilbur's language of "operating state" because, while it is descriptive of the beliefs and views held by an individual, it does not suppose any permanence or fixed position of logic but allows for the fluidity of movement into and out of states and speaks only to the operating assumptions in play at any given moment. In my experience, through my interviews and in my own observations, I have often seen individuals who at one point, while appearing to be operating from a more "advanced" logic, suddenly were thrown back to a more dualistic and simpler belief structure (stage) by some significant or impactful event. Stage theory, on the other hand, connotes linearity and a sense of irreversibility (as in "you cannot become 'un-enlightened'") and carries with it a perception of childlike immaturity to the earlier stages. Using the term operational states, refers simply to the predominate beliefs, experiences and ways of being that are in play at a given time, all of which include and add on to the previous basis of "facts" in one's lifetime of experience. Because this is more a scaffolding of one's conceptions, patterns of interaction and supporting belief systems, simpler operating states can and often do reappear later in life when a person is confronted with a significant trauma. What is altered and worked on in the dark night of the soul are the operational constructs (the attachments as John of the Cross calls them) from which one makes such meaning and understanding.

Fowler's schema, though ultimately portrayed as an upward spiral, focuses more on the logic platforms of each stage than on the shifts between stages

---

[185] Fowler is actually the source of the term "operating states" from his description of what is changing within and between his proposed stages. He states, "By now it should be clear that [one's] means changes in the *ways* or *operations* of faith knowing, judging, valuing and committing." (Fowler, *Stages of Faith*, 275.) Italics are his.

[186] Ken Wilber. *Integral Spirituality: A Startling New Role for Religion in the Modern and Postmodern World* (Boston: Shambhala Publications. Kindle Edition), Kindle Locations 290-293.

through the operating states, attributing the movement between stages in adulthood to what he calls "conversion and recapitulation."[187] A conversion, he says, occurs under the "claim of ultimacy" of a new logic or center of value wherein "we are made aware of previously unaware of but nonetheless powerful value centers."[188] But Bourgeault expresses movement through stages and states differently saying that the death/rebirth process is inclusive of itself. "As we evolve toward the Divine, we integrate and carry with us the consciousness gained at lower levels of being. We do not destroy or dissolve our lower nature. A part of us does not die so that another part of us can live. The *whole of us dies* at one level so that *the whole of us* is reborn at one level."[189] And that transitory whole which dies is what I would refer to as the operating states.

In the previous four chapters we see evidence of adults operating from a number of these different states. But what is missing is a systematic language to capture where and how these states operate logically. My proposed modification of Fowler's stages of faith is based both on the language of operational states observed in the spiritual journey, and the action of the dark night of the soul as the catalyst that causes this transformation. This, I believe is imperative for three reasons: First it is important to show how the perception and action of the dark night experiences not only cause changes in one's operating belief structure but also appear and function differently at each subsequent operational state.

Secondly, it is important to demonstrate the on-going and never ending nature of spiritual development. Fowler's populations may have been incomplete, as he admits, or more normative than he is willing to concede.[190] His intention was not in studying the effects of the dark night of the soul nor in identifying the specifics of how spirituality morphs or transforms across experiences, but rather to simply inventory and classify how persons described their spirituality, beliefs about religion (concepts like sin and God, etc.) and, like most theorists before him, overlay those observations on a chronological life line of linear maturation. Further, Fowler's interview protocol may not have been geared to discerning the full spectrum of changes in faith, theology and personal spirituality.[191]

Lastly, I believe it is important to identify the language of the individual on the path of spiritual development. Unless one recognizes that the believer will use different words, metaphors and logic to describe their emotions or the subject of their search, one would be misled in listening to their descriptions. What may

---

[187] Fowler, *Stages*, 275, 290.

[188] Fowler, *Stages*, 276.

[189] Bourgeault, *Wisdom Jesus*, 56.

[190] Fowler, *Stages*, 315.

[191] Fowler, *Stages*, 310-312.

sound like disdain or confusion from a traditional perspective of theology, may be no more than the seeker attempting to put into words that which s/he is experiencing while rejecting the nomenclature and rhetoric of a simpler, more dualistic theology.

Introduction to the Operating States

In studying the effects of the dark night experience, narratives seem to fall into two categories: those where the evolution and transformation of the believer's spirituality changes step-by-step with each successive experience of the dark night, and those wherein the transformation is reported as a whole. Whether these latter cases have lumped together multiple experiences as one or in fact endured one long, protracted dark night is irrelevant in that both groups ultimately end up operating from what would be described as a "non-dual" consciousness.

It may be helpful to think of the following less as a revamping of traditional stage theories and more like an observation of the ranges of how believers interact with theology, the scriptures and their beliefs. Think of this as walking into a gigantic church filled with people from every walk of life. As the minister reads the scripture for the day, or begins the sermon of the day, each person in the congregation will hear those words in a unique and individual way, based not so much on the words spoken but on the operating beliefs held by the individuals in the congregation. Just as that congregation is diverse by virtue of their education and life experiences, so are individuals scattered across a diverse spectrum of operating states by virtue of their encounter(s) within the dark night. Thus I believe that it will help shed light on where the spiritual seeker is in the process if we are able to provide a better description of the language and logic resulting from various operating beliefs.

Since it is my contention that operational states are fluid and hold within them elements of preceding "states" or structures of meaning making, sometimes severe or traumatic events in our lives can hurl us backward in our operational logic scheme, thus violating the linear concept of stage theory, as previously stated. For example, a person may be well advanced and operating at a high level of understanding when an event like Newtown CT or personal experience of discovering a cancerous tumor can result in thoughts of "why me," questions of theodicy, and beliefs that sound more like right/wrong duality which stage theorists claim is lost in childhood despite the fact that one often encounters otherwise intelligent and thoughtful persons who still cling to dualistic and literalistic beliefs.

As is the case in human development, spiritual progression or unfolding is more a result of reacting to external pressures and unresolvable problems than an act of choice or will, or as the result of the aging process. (In fact, willfulness is one of those things that gets blown up early on in the dark night). Fowler contends that during such time we seek to align ourselves with "a power sufficient enough to sustain us" and help us through such catastrophes.[192] His principle of recapitulation connotes that any traumatic event causes a re-evaluation of the former logic and a reshaping of that logic to conform to the newly-born operating state (my term).

In discussions with ministers participating in my survey, it appears more like the initial response to tragedy and trauma is not simply a recapitulation or review but rather a full return to the former state, and many times to fundamental dualism. For example one respondent discussing an incident of sexual harassment by her up-line administrator, went through a gamut of beliefs starting with feelings of being bad (am I bad - what did I do to deserve this?) to dualistic questions about God (how could a loving God allow this to happen?) Finding those fundamental beliefs to be equally inadequate to explain the situation, the individual then "tries on" several new belief structures until one is found that can accommodate the current reality and help "make sense" of it, eventually moving back to higher and more complex logic schemas or operating states. It is therefore the pressure of the catalytic event that forces movement (in both directions – toward duality and back toward non-duality) rather than the "claim of ultimacy" of the succeeding logic.

Since the research of Darwin on, we have found that our species has not evolved as a species because we wanted to, but rather because we must. Spiritual development is not a result of the inability of earlier, more simplistic levels of logic failing to hold or understand and resolve more complex life problems. It is a total collapse of the former belief structure under the weight of or necessity for dealing with one's current reality – we must find a resolution, least we go mad! Spiritual development according to Meister Eckhart is a process of subtraction. The more dualistic a belief system (i.e., right/wrong), the more rules need to be created to handle each situation (note the over 430 Mosaic laws of the early people in the Hebrew bible). The former logic must break down and be replaced by a logic and ethic that can allow for these more complex issues in life, with fewer rules, while still allowing for the existence of the previously held belief. Likewise, spiritual beliefs follow a process of unlayering as they encounter dealing with greater complexities. Both Loder and Fowler blur the lines of spiritual development with those of psychological or moral development. Loder claims:

> For this level of cognitive growth to become one's own style of thinking about oneself and one's world, it is argued that one must know suffering

---

[192] Fowler, *Stages*, 277.

and loss, responsibility and failure, and the grief that is an inevitable part of having made irreversible commitments of life's energy. This negative or dark side of human life is present from the beginning, but only at the middle years does it become patently plain that patterns of ego defense against this realization are gradually collapsing and giving way to the inevitable and ultimate triumph of negation that lies ahead.[193]

Loder seems to simply brush aside what we might view as precipitating events for the dark night of the soul and chalks up spiritual development as a by-product of the grief of losing one option by virtue of having chosen another or of the negativity of latent ego defenses. But here is where the dark night of the soul actually comes in. Dark nights are those places in our spiritual lives where the belief structure or ego defense structure, that once worked in dealing with people or protecting our ego, life and even the scriptures on a deeply personal/ethical (a.k.a. spiritual) level no longer work and must be supplanted. Because of the centrality of spiritual beliefs to the core of our being (at the soul level – or as psychology would say it, at the level of our fundamental understanding of self), these changes are experienced as radical and often psychologically painful transformations. Stage theories too often focus on building and the refinement of logic. But the refinement of operational states is subtractive starting from a place of separateness and difference (read that as having a set of beliefs in the uniqueness of the self as distinct from all else in the universe) *from* the almighty, and ultimately ending in a unitive place of oneness with all things *including* the almighty by virtue of losing all of the false distinctions created by the ego. Coming to know God through the dark night of the soul is a process of kenosis; of emptying oneself of everything – every thought, belief or supposed truth about the Divine – in order to allow the incarnation of the spirit of God within our very being. In the final chapter, I will discuss further how spirituality is altered after the dark nights of the soul.

In the following stage descriptions and summary table, some of the names given to the operating states are taken from both *Stages of Faith* and *The Logic of the Spirit* and incorporate some of Fowler's and Loder's language, but others include references I heard in the survey group with respect to the transformative results they experienced. Unlike Fowler's developmental model, operating states are not bound to ages or developmental stages. Furthermore, movement from one stage to the next should not be seen as a total abandonment of the previous stage. Wilbur calls this movement one of "transcend and include" since some vestiges of the previous states and stages are still retained at the next stage of logic. Put in

---

[193] Loder, *Logic of the Spirit*, 291.

Wilbur's terms, "the subject of one stage becomes the object of the next, thus owning but transcending that object, until – in an idealized sequence – all relative subjects and selves have been transcended and there is only one pure Witness or the Pure Self, the empty opening in which Spirit speaks."[194]

Descriptions in the chart are written in the first person singular to reflect what one might hear from a person operating at that level and to simplify the language in each cell. So with that allow me to introduce some of the nomenclature of the operational states:

- **Dualism** – We all start learning with labels and for the most part, this labeling exists as duality: good/bad; right/wrong; up/down and so on. Fundamentally Western logic (and the bulk of Western theology) is dominated by the dualism of the Greeks. But even the act of labeling a table and chair carries with it the thought that by calling it a chair we are meaning also that it is not table or any other non-chair type of item. In the narrative dialogues, this shows up as a kind of absolutism or certainty early in their discussion. It is a statement that "God is this" and not that. God is good and the devil is bad. It was the absolutism with which Mother Teresa and Karen Armstrong took their vows and the absolute zeal that drove Saul of Tarsus. At this point, sacred scriptures are absolute truths to be taken literally as dictated by God and transcribed by human hands.

- **Questioning Seeker** – Dualism has no room in it for questions. It explains all things: God is the source of all things good; the Devil is the source of all things bad. But contrarily, once a person begins to question "reality," the absolutism of dualism has to break up. At this state, there still exists an absolute right (God) and an absolute wrong (Devil) but there are now gradients and shades of goodness and badness. Psychologists call this state "multiplicity" for the multiple shades of gray. In the narratives, some of the participants referred to the areas of gray that caused them confusion. Operating from the point of Questioning Seeker allows for doubt to take center stage. The Questioning Seeker says, "I know that there must be a God, but I am no longer certain what that is or what God looks like."

- **Called** – At some point in one's spiritual life, a distant (duality-based) God becomes personal and real – one has an experience or felt perception of personal connection. At first blush, this is a feeling of being deeply, and unconditionally loved. We feel touched and even called by name by God, Spirit, the Divine, or Higher Power (we each give it our own name as the process is so personal). To some degree we are all called

---

[194] Wilbur, *Integral Spirituality*, Kindle location 2418.

by God, though not everyone experiences that as a call into the ministry. We begin looking at others in terms of their spiritual nature as well – "are they one of us or not" (note the residual duality still living in that question?). Operating from a state of being called places the Seeker in relationship with God wherein decisions are no longer made by the "small self" alone, but are inclusive of the soul or big SELF. Elements of small egoic self are lost in the context of "What would God have me do, or what would Jesus do?" However, we need only look to the disciples to see that simply the act of being called or feeling called is not sufficient to cause a full transformation of dualistic logic into unitive or non-dual logic. I even suspect that the stories of their folly, their flawed logic and their failures in the times of trial are given to us so that we can identify with the disciples as chosen and on the path despite the fact that our small self is still in control.

•   **Committed** – Having experienced the touch of the Divine, at some point one must make a choice. "If I have been called, then to what am I called?" Taking a stand as a called and spiritually-centered human is a risk and carries with it the potential for becoming unwelcome, outcast or at times just held at arms length from others. It is a feeling of having lost one's personal life goals and having had those replaced by a greater purpose. It is the responsibility Weems talked of having lost when she hit a period of unbelief. Her roles as professor, researcher and minister carried not only commitments but also ways of being on which she relied.

•   **Accountable** – This is where the "rubber meets the road;" where the operating state that drives a person gains traction in confronting and dealing with the issues of the world. Are you really a faith-based person? The universal law of physics – which states that for every action there is an *equal* and *opposite* reaction – will test one's commitments and accountability through equally powerful and "negative" events. The very act of making a hard-and-fast commitment opens one's eyes to the barriers and obstacles that will confront and stall that commitment. The burden of carrying the weight of the world often brings the accountable person to their knees. One of the ministers in the survey group referred to this when s/he said, "I thought I knew what I had been called to but it seemed as though God kept upping the ante on me till I felt I could not handle it by myself. I just wasn't enough – not strong enough, spiritual enough, compassionate enough." In truth this awareness brings one to the brink of surrendering individual effort and to falling into trusting and relying on God.

- **Conjunctive Non-Duality** – Duality finally loses its stronghold on logic and life and the world becomes visible in terms of "both…and" (hence Fowler's term "conjunctive") understanding. What seemed paradoxical is now seen as part of a greater whole or included within the other. However the last duality to fall is the Divine/human separation. People like those in the survey begin talking about the loss of meaningful boundaries – not in the negative psychopathological sense – but as a sense of oneness with others and others' struggles, pains and life situations. This is the state that FitzGerald describes as understanding ourselves as "we poor" and "we oppressed." Others are objective until the distinction of separateness and uniqueness falls in Conjunctive Non-Duality. And we see ourselves as separate from God (and see God as an object of our quest and of our love) until we discover the reality of incarnation – that there is no separation between God and SELF, that God has bridged that divide and that the in-dwelling God reveals our divine nature as well.

- **Constructivism/Authorship** – Once duality is erased (and one names one's own Christ consciousness, "I and the father are one"), one begins to understand that one's experienced "reality" is in actuality a fabrication of the mind and ego based on the limited subset of available human experiences and that our true SELF is in God living through us. If that be the case, then is it possible for us to become co-author of our life experiences with God? We realize that we have created God in our image and now have no idea of who/what God is – only THAT God is. "This is the grand, irreversible figure-ground shift," says Loder, "in which our entire developing life, the whole of the life span, and the totality of one's own existence, moves into the background and the Creator Spirit becomes the central figure, the definitive reality."[195] [196]

- **Detachment/Servitude** – As we become co-authors of our life in God, our ego and willfulness finally move aside for God and divine purpose. All intellectual activity must be left behind as one realizes it's downfall in trying to master by understanding. We let go of all judgments, labels, and presuppositions and allow God to shape us. We become an instrument, a vessel, and a channel for divine purpose. Mother Teresa put this nicely when she wrote, "He can do with me as it pleaseth Him, without even a thought of consulting me … I will be happy to be just

---

[195] Loder, *Logic of the Spirit*, 248.

[196] Contrary to Loder, however, I do not hold the belief that it is irreversible. Even beyond this point, our little self, out private ego has a nasty habit of attempting to slip back into the control seat and interpret life on its own terms.

nothing and He everything."[197] Small self is no longer in the driver's seat, in fact small self becomes only a nagging whisper in the background to which we no longer need listen.

•   **Universalizing/Relativism** – The more we come to know God in this journey, the more we understand how little our experience has actually shown us. We stand in awe before the vastness of what we do not and cannot understand and yet which defines our very being. All knowledge is minute in relation to what is. All knowledge – that is, all and anything we can be capable of knowing – is finite as defined by time, place and experience, and the overwhelming realization at this point is that such experiences are just peeks and glimpses of whatever is at their source. We know without knowing while understanding that we ultimately have no clue of what it is we claim to know. We are utterly humbled by that. Laws and logic are supplanted by an inner gyroscope that seems to continually right our course bearing and steer us toward the more effective and useful path. "Holiness is not keeping the commandments: it is making them unnecessary."[198] It is that state that Paul described in Romans chapter 7, that he had died to the law and yet believed the law to be holy and good. Yet that notwithstanding, there is a sense that this is only the beginning, that there are yet other deaths and rebirths to come.

The following two-page chart details how an individual's operating system views self, God, power, logic, prayer and relationships change as a result of the action and effect of the dark night of the soul. Columns across the top of the two pages represent the evolution of the nine operating states (starting from the left) and the rows labeled down the left side are provided to show how those different operating states perceive and interact in various elements of the human experience. Each cell contains only a phrase or sentence describing how that aspect of the world is seen, and is in no way meant to be complete. Teresa of Avila pictured her inward journey as entering a large castle with many rooms – each successive one being contained within the previous. Rather than viewing the following chart as a linear progression, I think of it much more like Teresa's Interior Castle only proceeding from left to right instead of moving to the center. Our first and fundamental experience of God and of faith is in the left most column and progression of operating complexity increases to the right and second page.

---

[197] Kolodiejchuk, *Mother Teresa*, 284.

[198] Loder, *Logic of the Spirit*, 308.

The chart is reflective of anecdotal descriptions is presented in an effort to capture and organize some of the changes heard in the survey population. While the chart is based in and expands on the existing stage theory, it is not based on empirical data or research. It is presented in the hopes that it may provide a helpful vocabulary and framework for dealing with what happens in and through the dark nights of the soul.

Operating States	Unconscious Dualism	Questioning Seeker	Called	Committed
	1	2	3	4
Experience of God and God's Power	God is "out there" all-powerful Sky God: I can only ask and hope; life is pre-ordained and predestined.	How is / How can God be concerned with me? Where is God in my life?	I understand God's presence as a personal spiritual experience: I hear and discern God's voice	I am God's and God is mine. I happily proclaim God's love as real and palpable in all of life. I feel called by God
Concept of Self	My body and my self-image are who I am. Pleasuring and protecting myself is of prime importance - Undifferentiated self	My external behavior is who I am. I must defend my actions as original, mine and blameless. It is all about looking good. Magical beliefs	My thoughts and feelings are who I am. This is not an enlightenment but rather the beginning of individuation and separation. Being called sets me apart. Mythic reality	My deeper intuitions are a guide to who I am. Self-centeredness has failed me and exposed self-referential, and self-centered righteousness as folly. Who am I really? Rational level of group consciousness
Form of Logic/Moral Judgment	Dualistic, good/bad; right/ wrong. God and Devil constitute the source of morality and truth	Multiplistic - shades of right and wrong but still an ultimate God/Devil polarity; If God is all-powerful, why does evil and tragedy exist?	Contextual and relative to situation. Forms of nihilism (there is no ultimate right/ wrong duality) but I can pray and choose	Situations and circumstances no longer determine what I do; My commitment to the path is the sole determinant
Source of Personal Power	Power is external to me; Life is experienced in reactions only; I am a pawn or victim	Insightful questioning leads to recognition of when I am on purpose or off purpose; seeking new solutions	Power begins to shift internal; Self worth derives from being touched and held by God	Focus and resoluteness of my convictions are "senior" to personal circumstances; "saying so" causes things to happen
Nature of Prayer	Need fulfillment: often ego driven petitions	Conversations with God - who are you God and what am I?	Confessions of unworthiness: shape me and mold me	Surrender - trying to listen for and discern God's instruction
Relation to Scripture	Scripture is absolute and infallible word of God, literalist reading is the only option	See the scripture as holding answers to life's questions	God talks to me through the scriptures	The practice of Lectio Divina takes on guiding power as the *effect* of the reading over and above the literal meaning of the words
Relation to Other People	There are only two camps in the world - those who are for me and those against me	I look for alignment and others who are asking similar questions	Interacting and influencing others by the passion I have for my stand or my calling	I am able to put a cause in motion through interactions with others
Locus of Authority	Little power to change anything; my best skill is able to be okay with reacting to the now	I can be the "swing" vote; can add my voice to (voting for or against) the mass of what defines "what is"	I can convince others of the unique interpretation I have of certain "facts"	View people's reactions as "results" generated and modify my actions to produce greater effectiveness
Concept of Sin	I am sinful and there is nothing I can do about it; I can only try to get it right and adhere to the laws. If I am good I will be rewarded.	Pray for forgiveness: a contrite heart will win grace	We are a fallen people saved by grace alone	God has called each of us to step forward through and despite our sins
Action of the Dark Night	Failure of religious beliefs to help in any way; anger at God for allowing me to suffer	God has withdrawn from me - I am being punished for my transgressions	Vulnerability; not only am I exposed in my nakedness, but I have no control of when this happens	Spiritual dryness; prayer and worship have no effect; sense of asking "why me Lord?"
Impact of the Dark Night of the Soul	Fear, fright and physical pain. Devastating onslaughts of the devil; tormenting and painful loss of being	Sudden loss of the connection to/with God; identification with Job and the Psalms of lament	Aloneness and nakedness in the face of my calling; renewed questioning "are you there for me Lord?"	I learn that prayer is not for God - prayer changes the pray-er; I cannot use another's words and must come to God on my own

Figure 4. Operational States and the Effect of the Dark Night of the Soul

Accountable	Conjunctive Non-Duality	Constructivism/Authorship	Detachment/Servitude	Universalizing/Relativity
5	6	7	8	9
Others know my God because of how I show up; pastoral responsibility is not deterred or swayed by external events and circumstances	God has bridged the human/divine gulf; incarnation means living with and within the Divine; I surrender to Divine flowing through me	Understanding that all concepts and experiences of God are limited by and to the extent of personal vocabulary and range of experience	Can functionally let go of all preconceived notions and feelings relating to the experience of God; God is source and ground of all being	Understanding that all experience and beliefs of God are merely relative to the reality they represent; the more I experience of God the more unfathomable God becomes
My shadow self is who I am. Everything so far is exposed as a cover-up for my shadow self. This is where you meet your raw, unpolished self as it is, and as God sees it.	I am nothing and powerless to save myself. "I" no longer exists separate from the Divine, and is swallowed up in the greater whole.	I am so much more than who/what I thought I was. I am revealed as a channel for Divine Love. I am in God and God lives in me, but it is no longer about me.	Inner-most self is seen to be God, the ever-present outpouring of incomprehensible loving. The non-dual self recognizes all distinctions as passing names for convenience	I am that I am. I am indistinguishable from all else and all else from me and yet, in the moment, able to be fully present to that which I am as I am. I am love incarnate for the sole purpose of reuniting infinite love with itself
My personal commitment means nothing unless it is seen through the effect on others. "Pastoral" leadership is evident through those moved by my actions	Duality is replaced by "both/and" and contrarian views are seen as part of the greater whole of understanding. Knowing starts moving from head to heart	Recognition that I can never really "know" anything as absolute; freedom from "should" "is." "Factuality"& "absoluteness" of any construct disappears and allows reality to reveal to me what it intends	View innocent suffering as a call to work for justice: see a path, solution, or course of action where none existed before. Inner knowing beyond factual knowing - trusting heart wisdom	Paradox and mystery are the state of things enjoyed for the beauty and energy they produce in the spaces in between. Logic of the mind no longer rules knowing. Mind is entrained to heart.
Truth telling (what really are my results?) brings clarity to my commitment and strength of my conviction and "yes" to the journey	Able to see the truth in others' reality as part of the whole; Truth has no bounds and has room for all; Increased ability to "enroll" others without judgment or confrontation	The world of "possibilities" no longer exist as "probability estimates" but as actual alternative paths I could take, I become co-author of my own reality and destiny with and in partnership with God	Since God is all and in through and with all life, my life itself is best expressed in full and complete service to others; "little self" has died to "Self" in Christ/God	A feeling of timelessness and boundless energy when being "on purpose" or working on a higher purpose
A lack of questions to ask; surrendering even knowing and wanting to know	Contemplative prayer and meditation: prayer becomes wordless	Contemplation and meditation are grounding processes for daily living	A feeling of God "praying" me. Tonglun - ability to hold and heal the pain of the world.	Everything becomes prayer - even breathing, living in constant conscious contact, praying with every moment.
I have a responsibility to discern historical story and mythology from commandments and guidance in the scripture	Scripture I no longer absolute and infallible; contradictions are easily understood as the process of human translation or chronicling errors	Full midrashic understanding of scripture as contextual, spiritual and ethical meanings relative to my own unfolding ability to understand	Passion for the beauty of certain portions or books of the Bible; see the wisdom of the literature as transcending the biblical context.	Understanding of the parables and paradoxes not for the story they tell but for the effect they cause
View people as the focus of overall effectiveness and purpose of my commitments	Boundaries and barriers between self and others fall away; exclusivity disappears	Compassion for others because of seeing the dual bind of their own self-imposed constraints; pointing the way	Feeling of being drawn into service where it is most needed irrespective of circumstances. Understanding of others' POV even my enemies'.	Willingness to die, spiritually or physically even to protect the life on an enemy; my life is expendable at the higher plane of morality
Can influence others less focused or committed; and can hold ground with other committed leaders	Influence and authority "over" anything is lost and meaningless. "I" disappear from the equation	Ability to let the future speak into my reality, a sense of seeing all things for what they really are	Confidence of Romans 8:37-39, that there is nothing in the universe that can separate me from the love of God	Understanding of a higher, universal ethic that supersedes all temporal laws
Our fallibility and fallenness are natural elements of humanity; forgiveness has been granted before we sin	Living in the grace and understanding that Jesus did not have to die for us to be saved	Understanding that the sin is not in the deed but in the thought before the deed.	The sole source of sin and sinfulness is egoic disconnection from the Divine source of love.	Sin as the result of eating of the fruit of the tree of knowledge. The presumption of knowing other, self or God is the definition of sin.
A second wave of fear and fearfulness; thoughts that I had this handled and a way to do it are dashed to the ground. This the "night of the senses."	Feeling totally ripped open and eviscerated; the pain of the world hits harder than any of my own pains; pure "spiritual madness" and "night of the spirit."	Contemplative prayer and meditation are the places where I meet God to come and listen; a sense of God at work in me beyond my knowing	Least I get blasé in my wordless feeling of presence, dark nights come as a not-so-gentle reminder to wake up and stay awake	Every night is another dark night, every dark corner is a place to look for light; light is most noticeable in the darkest places
Recognition of the pattern: "here it comes again" and ownership of the ego's role in losing communion with God	Understanding that dark nights are a part of the process of spiraling in and out of understanding and connectivity; spirituality has an ebb and flow	Experiences become wordless and concept-less; Indescribable presence of God; sense that no one will understand what I went or am going through	Loss of ego; feeling totally emptied, burned up or consumed by the fire; my life is given for the service it can produce in others	Recognition of the divinity of all life; loss of judgments, labels and expectations; deep compassion for all life including enemies

Figure 4 (*cont'd*). Operational States and the Effect of the Dark Night of the Soul

What must be understood about this system of operating states, however, is that there is absolutely no "value" or "level" difference between a person who operates at a fundamental dualistic perspective and one whose operational state is more universalizing. Insofar as belief in God is concerned, one state is no better than another; one is no worse than any other. Any and all of these operating states are systems of logic that put the believer in touch with the reality of God *as God appears to that believer at that time*. That one person's experience has caused a breakdown of one's previously functional operating state and forced another to grow in its place does not result in that person being in a better place from which to understand God (that of which one is ultimately incapable of understanding). Each operating state is fully functional in dealing with life, death, and the mysteries of the Divine as they appear to that state of consciousness.

Along the way, it may appear to an individual that "surely this way of thinking is 'better' than how I was thinking or believing before." However, over time one sees that each operating state in turn must die to itself in order to make way for the next operating state to grow. So that even at a state of universalizing, one sees the impermanence of every operating system (even this one) as the one common characteristic. If one holds on to the belief that universalizing/relativism is "the" state, that belief will ultimately result in the demise of its own functionality. In fact, one finally arrives at a compassion for all of the operating states as still living and at times functioning within oneself and one's belief system and an unnerving sense that there is more. And at the same time, one realizes that through the process of "transcend and include," one may still hold a dualistic, right/wrong belief that (for example) killing is bad or wrong in any circumstance.

The understanding of different levels of operational states is not simply my ideal but rather a direct application of what Jesus said in John 14:2, "In my Father's house are many dwelling places." To me this could easily be describing the operational states; that in God, there is room for everyone to be, however they happen to be "being" or operationally understanding their connection.

The only problem that can and often does occur within the earlier operational states (1 through 5) is when, or if, any one state vilifies another's belief structure or elevates its own, as frequently is the case among persons operating from a more dualistic state. Dualism, by its very nature, creates a false illusion of "is/is not," and if that duality is held within a strongly polarized valuing structure, the "is not" can be significantly devalued to the point of seeming evil or wrong.[199] As dualism breaks down and gives way to multiplisitc and eventually non-dual forms of logic what evolves is a compassionate understanding of, and inclusion of, the other operating states. One can see in oneself those places where one still holds fast to a dualistic operational belief. What is always true of transformation, as I have already stated, is that the former beliefs are not obliterated but held for the value that they represented (or still represent) and transformed into the more inclusive system of understanding. There is still room for an inclusion of the previously held operating states.

In Jesus we have not only a model of one operating at a fully universalizing state, but also an brilliant example of his inclusiveness of anyone operating at other states. Ultimately, even Jesus recognized that to access the relationship with divine love at an even "higher" level, he (take that also as his current operating reality) would have to die. Time and again his followers asked questions informed by the logic of dualism, called or committed states, but he gently answers them and provides the next course correction to that logic. Jesus was well schooled in the scriptures and the teachings of the rabbinic sages of the first century BCE. Following after him, Paul and Peter took up the charge of teaching from this enlightened, operational state. One can see evidence in Paul's writing of his shifts between differing operational logic schemes, including times of reverting to a "lower" operational state. The net result of enduring the dark nights of the soul is seen as a progression across the previous chart and ultimately results in a transformed spirituality.

---

[199] We see this evident in the numerous dualistic religious sects that seek to vilify all "non-believers."

Chapter Six – Penu-el: A Theology of the Dark Night

Then Jacob said to him, "Please tell me your name." But he said, "Why is it that you ask me my name?" And there he blessed him. So Jacob called the place Penuel (face of El) saying, "For I have seen God face to face and yet my life is preserved." The sun rose on him has he passed Penuel, limping because of his hip.

Genesis 32: 29-31 (New Oxford Annotated Bible)

So, once we have met the Son,
We are tempted ever after to pray to the Father,
'Lead us into temptation and evil for our sake.'
They will come, all right, don't worry; probably in a form
That we do not expect, and certainly with a force
More dreadful than we can imagine.[200]

W.H. Auden

Across the ages, human experience has provided the structure and back-story for theology and the experience of God. Our language, the predominate philosophy of the time and our personal life experience have all played an integral part in shaping the precepts and principles of traditional Christian theology; a theology which had been created in a static world and based on an outmoded cosmology that is no longer relevant in our times.[201] In recent years, theology has begun shucking those previously held notions to make way for a more integrative theology of the new millennium.[202] Modern science, physics, astronomy and mathematics have reduced the Genesis story for most, and even the opening chapter of the Gospel according to John for some, to mythical allegory. Likewise, the dark night of the soul, as a significant personal experience, often drastically impacts one's perception of God, the way in which one reads scripture, and one's personal stance on theology as our operating system moves from a dualistic to a non-dual, unitive stance. As a result of the dark night words (even sacred words) are quite often rendered empty and meaningless; long-held beliefs become myths and stories; seemingly all is called into question and no stone is left unturned. But then what remains of one's theology and belief system when that which one has been taught is brought under the light? In this chapter, I shall attempt to unravel the old and reweave a new fabric of faith that appears to hold together at this point in my spiritual journey. While proper attribution is made where called for, the bulk of this chapter consists of my personal theological perspective having been one of those travelers through the dark night of the soul.

---

[200] WH Auden "A Christmas Oratorio" (1941), Accessed March 22, 2008, from http://southerncrossreview.org/44/auden-oratio.htm

[201] Ilia Delio, *Christ in Evolution* (Orbis Books, Kindle Edition, 2011), Kindle location 624-625.

[202] Ilia Delio's brilliant presentation of the structure of a new, science-compatible theology starts with Teilhard de Chardin's claim that religion has calcified and become "fossilized," and weaves together strands from Panikkar, Rahner, and Moltmann to create a sound if not profound understanding of a cosmic Christ for today.

Above all, the theology of the dark night must have a clear and definable structure if it is to become valid. Not only is it grounded in God and seeking union with the ineffable source of infinite love, the theology of the dark night sees Jesus as its prime leader by example. While not concerning itself with either Jesus's divinity or humanity, dark night theology looks first at the action that love calls one to do.

Toward a Theology of the Dark Night

Every theological system has an ontological beginning and an eschatological end game - an alpha and omega - a source and a direction. For the theology of the dark night, these blend together in love. Love, a feeling of first being loved, created in love and held in love is where it all begins, and dissolving into unitive love, becoming one with the divine love that is the beingness and nature of God, is its only finality. In this way the beginning sets in place a quest for the endpoint. The theology of the dark night is far less concerned with Christology than it is with living the principles taught by Jesus. It starts with an assumption of God as the source of this love, and neither deifies Jesus nor concerns itself with his humanity. The theology of the dark night is a theology of praxis (as Armstrong discovered – an orthopraxy not orthodoxy). The theology of the dark night is diametrically opposed to the popular thought that one should not trust one's "gut." Recitation of creeds and memorized liturgies sometimes remove us from our personal mystical knowing. Whereas Jesus often told those he healed that their "faith had made them whole/" Their practice of stepping into and trusting their own experience was what he praised and reinforced each time, likewise, one who has gone through the dark night of the soul has a faith based not in fact but in the deep-seated feeling of their soul's experience. Having repeatedly walked through the dark night where the only bearings one has are the feelings of presence or absence of God, one learns to trust this internal gyroscope of faith above any written cannon.

God is. By virtue of the fact that every culture in the history of humanity, predating even the development of agriculture, has born evidence of having struggled to name the inescapable awareness of something greater than ourselves, I am certain that the one constant in our human experience is this higher power we refer to as "God." But coming to "know" God (as much as one can) is not an easy business, and the crafting of a religious doctrine is flawed from the first step forward. Religious insights and assumptions are not self-evident as some might claim. Yet despite that, the pursuit of a definitive theological system has filled more texts over time than perhaps any other single subject. How can we come to any knowledge of such a thing when we cannot see it or name it – yet just as surely cannot escape its ever-present touch? God ultimately refuses to be known.

From the beginning, when Moses asked God who he was, God's answer was essentially, "Never mind that, I am who I am!"[203]

Traditional theology often approaches the issue of defining God by what God is not, like Elijah knowing that God was not present in the firestorm or the earthquake, or it approaches from a description of the identifiable characteristics of God, creating a language of superlatives – omnipresence, omniscience, etc. – to describe the supreme nature of the Divine. These two approaches, emanating respectively from eastern orthodoxy and western monastic studies, pushed human understanding to great depths or heights as the case might be: eastern apophatic thought to an empty silence of contemplation and western cataphatic thought to the lofty adoration and the canonization of saintly living. Each was correct and yet, in approaching the Divine, always fell short. Like Heisenberg's uncertainty principle shows, the more precise the focus is on one side the more uncertain our understanding of the other becomes. So the problem might lie in our conceptualization itself. Our struggle to place actuality and discreteness on God is a contradiction in terms. Our individual revelations may be real experiences of God, but as soon as these are elevated to the level of conceptual theology, they become rational abstractions. Both approaches focused perhaps too much on the intellectual realm. So what then of the human spiritual experience?

The journey of spirituality is a journey toward oneness with the Divine. In making that journey what has to be realized is not the greatness of the Divine but rather the false illusion of the self as distinct and different from the Divine. The inward journey of spirituality is a death spiral of the false self – falling into the true SELF or greater self, which is God. But in getting to this sense of unity and oneness we come to realize that not only has the false self (the ego) set up a false boundary between itself and God, but it has also constructed that same boundary between itself and all else. If incarnation has one thing to teach us it is that we and the creator are one selfsame being.[204] And by extension, while distinct and separate, we are also one with all creation.

To get to this point requires a "deconstruction" of the false self. The truth taught by nearly all mystics (especially in the Buddhist tradition) is that the illusion of self as distinct from other is not only a contrivance of the mind, it is the source of all suffering: from the existential pain of aloneness to the gut-wrenching resentments that become anger, hatred and prejudice. The practices outlined by John of the Cross, the unknown author of *The Cloud of Unknowing*, Ignatius

---

[203] Karen Armstrong, *The Case for God* (New York: Anchor Books, 2010), 39.

[204] This does not mean that God in any way "looks" or acts like we human creatures of God. One common fallacy of primitive religious constructs was to ascribe human qualities, emotions and logic to the Divine. Rather the recognition that one is a participant in the Divine oneness is what is meant by I am in God and God is in me.

Loyola and so many other Christian mystics, while described in a time before psychology had even begun to articulate a theory of the ego and unconscious, are designed to pull down these presumed barriers between self and other and between self and God.

The deconstruction of the false self is the process of recognizing that our investment in the states, and accomplishments – the false identities – with which we complete the sentence "I am…" are the illusions of the ego or false self (e.g., I am a male, I am a champion, I am a Christian, I am a psychologist, and so on). When these attributes dissolve into the nothingness that they are, we arrive simply at the sentence, "I am." Thus the "I am" is the only true and essential self and the net result of the inward journey. Is it then any wonder that we come to God, the one whose proclamation of existence was "I am who I am," when we strip ourselves of the attributes of ego-identity?

Perhaps when Jesus said "I and the father are one" he was not claiming his unique divinity as separate from our humanness, but rather making a profound proclamation that when one divests oneself of the illusions of "thingness," one comes to the core and essential self of "I am" and therefore oneness with the great "I am" that is the source of all creation. Thus at the end of the inward spiritual journey lies this truth that "I and the creator are one," and that "I (too) am who I am." It is the core truth of Jullian of Norwich who is said to have run through the streets shouting, "My innermost being is God." "If we draw close to the roots of our existence, to the naked being of our self, we will find ourselves at that point where God and ourselves unite in ontological communion."[205] Merton called it the virginal point, where the soul is untouched and untouchable by anyone except the perfect love of God.

How this transpires in through the dark night might be described as a process of kenosis and incarnation. The kenotic process of passing through the dark night of the soul prepares us by emptying oneself of the trappings and attachments of the ego such that, as an emptied vessel we personally can be filled by God and become the incarnation of the spirit/word made flesh in our very being.

What Jesus, as *the* incarnation example, modeled so well was this selfless emptying that allowed him to be the embodiment of the Divine – of God's very presence in the fullness of human form. Paul, himself a traveler of the dark night of the soul, gave us a clue as to how this happens in Philippians 2:6-11. "Although He existed in the form of God, He did not regard equality with God a thing to be grasped, but emptied Himself, taking the form of a bond-servant, *and* being made in the likeness of men. Being found in

---

[205] Finley, *Merton's Palace*, 136.

appearance as a man, He humbled Himself by becoming obedient to the point of death, even death on a cross." The operative verbs in that early hymn, though, are "emptied" and "humbled." Jesus' message was not that it was an exclusive state that he and he alone could manifest. Rather he consistently taught that it was who and what we were to be as well. *We* need to be emptied and humbled in order to fully receive the in-flowing of God's love as the incarnation within.

However, we must understand that the process is not a one-way street. We continually need to empty ourselves so that we can be filled by the enfleshment of the word. The ego never totally dies or goes away – really (though anthropomorphically speaking, it *thinks* it is dying!). Rather, the ego is emptied out through each time that the soul realizes that once again ego is full of itself by having laid claim to the experience of God as the actuality of God or by simply, like Peter, wanting to stay there and build an altar. So we go back and forth over the threshold of incarnation and death until perhaps some day when we fully empty ourselves in our final physical death.

However, the kenosis, the emptying of self/ego, whether through contemplative practices or through the pain of realizing that once again one has lost conscious contact with the Divine source of love, and the subsequent "dark night" that triggers, is the only way to "clear the way for the Lord in the wilderness; Make smooth in the desert a highway for our God," as Isaiah said. (Is. 40:3) Through this continual process we can experience the incarnation of the word in ourselves, becoming one with God to complete the couplet "I am in God *AND* God is in me." As the dark night continues to empty us we make inner space to recognize how God is filling us. When egoic fear gives way to trust in God, we no longer fear that the emptying will result in our nothingness but in fact will result in our realization of being filled with and by the Divine.

The great caveat which comes with striving to be one with God is that this also makes me one with all else. Our conventional worldview is one of fragmentation and separateness. We falsely believe that we are different from and separate from "them," whoever "they" might be (criminals, politicians, liars, Baptists, Buddhists, people of different skin color – the list goes on *ad infinitum*). We further extrapolate this belief to include the rest of creation, believing that we are separate from the planet on which we live and the biosystem which sustains us. And our collective separations have resulted in killing each other and in killing off our host environment.

But when the boundary is made permeable (and eventually dissolves through the dark night) we can no longer deny our connection with all else in creation. Our own participation in divinity means that all else and all other is equally a part of the Divine. In losing the false self, we are broken open by love and compelled to embrace everyone – the sinners and saints alike – as equally divine and sacred. We are forced to see the Divine in all things. And when the constructed boundaries dissolve we can even recognize the divinity of the spaces in between. Christ, as incarnation, is not a static, historical event, claims Teilhard. Christ is an on-going cosmic unfolding through all of creation – not exclusive to Christians, or just believers, or only human beings in this particular solar system. Christ is the universal incarnation that is the expression of God as the creative force – continually, and forever coming into being as the totality of creation.[206]

A Theology of Praxis

But it is not sufficient to say that the theology that emerges from the dark night of the soul is or is not concerned with definitions, distinctions and dogmatic credo. It is a theology based in the *acts* of love – having been loved and thus becoming an expression of that love. Two things happen in that process. The first is that having experienced that deep and unconditional love in the first place puts a force in motion within the beloved. Not only has the Divine/human boundary been destroyed but the boundary between self and all else has fallen as well. From that place of unity one is called to be a channel of divine love and loving, to be the new incarnation reaching out in compassion to those most thirsting for love – the "untouchables" of society. No longer seeing a distinction between "we" and "they" opens up a two-way street. The heart broken open by this love has been humbled to equality with the poorest, and meekest of society, yes, but at the very same time that open heart suddenly feels all the pain and suffering of those peoples with whom one has identified in saying, "we poor, we suffering, we oppressed."

The second action resulting from being broken open by love is that one can therefore no longer remain passive as an observer of oppression. There is a sudden and clear recognition of the fact I, and those others whom I perceive, are one in communion with the same whole. "As long as I do not open my heart and do not see that the other is not an other but a part of myself who enlarges and completes me, I will not arrive at dialogue."[207] Jesus never ministered to the elite and the privileged. He never preached from the pulpit. His ministry was a ministry of the streets, to and for the oppressed and hungry. His consistent message was that only the poor, the oppressed, the downtrodden, the widows and those in suffering could hear his message. And Jesus consistently preached that words without action are meaningless. The seeker who has gone through the dark

---

[206] Delio, *Christ in Evolution*, Kindle location 1356-1357.
[207] Delio, *Christ in Evolution*, Kindle Location 1867-1868.

night understands what that means. It is a message that can only be understood in the dark, and as a result of deep suffering.

Christian theology without praxis ceases to be Christian just as much as Christian praxis without theology ceases to be Christian. I am not contending that as a result of the dark night's baptism one simply goes into action; it must be based in an understanding of God as infinite love. The action (and the word praxis is used to express a conscientious and intentional type of action) is grounded in God and is a kenotic, emptying of one's love on and for others. This emptying, this giving of oneself is not pedantic or patronizing, but rather a recognition of the presence of God in the connection between two or more people. Delio writes, "The deep "I" of the spirit, of solitude and of love, cannot be "had," possessed, developed, perfected. It can only be, and act according to deep inner laws which are not of man's contriving but which come from God... This inner "I" who is always alone is always universal: for in this inmost "I" my own solitude meets the solitude of every other man [sic.] and the solitude of God. Hence it is beyond division, beyond limitation, beyond selfish affirmation."[208] When the element of God in me encounters the element of God in another, the spark that flashes in that coming together is the manifestation of a greater mass of the (two or more) elements of the Divine – a fuller and more complete feeling of the presence of God. "Where two or more are gathered in his name" no longer represents a quorum worthy enough to be visited by some wandering God, or a minyan sufficient to turn God's head, but they, that is the gathered relationship, are the very essence of God itself.

In my undergraduate days I lived in a house of nine pre-seminarians whose communal life was based on Dietrich Bonheoffer's *Life Together*. We called it a "faith and life" community because of Bonheoffer's contention that one's identity is only formed in community and that one's spirituality, by extrapolation, must always be held within some greater socio-ethical context.[209] Christianity is shared and must be lived communally on a daily basis. That is the message of Jesus in saying, "follow me." It was not a "follow me on a pilgrimage," "follow me to a church worship service," or "follow me into the desert." Jesus was setting the example to follow him into the crowds, into the street, among the lepers, with the women and children. "Follow me" into relationship with those who have no one. "Follow me" even into death.

---

[208] Delio, *Christ in Evolution*, Kindle location 2031-2035.

[209] Despite every effort I cannot place a finger on the passage in *Life Together* that is the origin of that thought, and must have come to that conclusion through our many late night discussions with my housemates or our spiritual advisor, H. Frederick Reisz.

But we first must be made poor; we need to be made humble (maybe even to be humiliated) and emptied in order to be in a position to see and hear the message of universal love and become its expression. From a position of unexamined and entrenched privilege we cannot see beyond our accomplishments and our pride. It is through the experience of the dark night that the illusion of having accomplished good deeds, of having won whatever status we have, and even of having defined and come to understand ourselves, as we know ourselves is exposed as the false idol of the ego. With our egoic golden calf melted down and ground into a fine powder we have a chance to drink in the truth and to understand the message of God's love. The transformation that occurs in the dark night of the soul is not only a transformed way of seeing, but a transformed state of being. All that mattered to the ego has been revealed as false and irrelevant. All that matters in the morning after the dark night is compassion. But compassion is only real when it is born from suffering, humility and poverty. The dark night strips our egos of any pretense of "suchness" until we lay naked and hungry in the gutter from which point we can see eye to eye with the poor and down trodden.

Truth is no longer a mere metaphysical hermeneutic with which our beliefs may or may not correspond. Instead, after the dark night of the soul, truth aspires to becoming real through praxis. Theology no longer merely reflects upon the world but is insistent (maybe even urgent) on becoming part of the process through which the world itself is transformed.

In the last days of his life Jesus gave us two examples of how to follow him: the last supper and the crucifixion. If one were to blend the two together in analysis, one sees that, in the crucifixion, Jesus handed his body over to the power elite in a supreme gesture of kenosis. In a sense he was saying, "you cannot kill me unless I first give myself up to you to be killed." In a very similar fashion, Jesus broke the bread and gave it to his followers as if it were his body being given over. To whom? To men and women who were concerned more with power and power struggles than with the message of their leader.[210] But like the crucifixion, being given and eating that bread is a radical destruction of their systems of power and our reliance on power. Jesus' followers needed and wanted a messiah, a conquering king who would restore the reign of God to its rightful place of dominance. But Jesus knew messianic hope to be a false power and turned it upside down in using the most common elements of a meal to describe what real power was.[211] Real power comes from the bottom – not top down; real

---

[210] Even at the last supper, the disciples were more concerned with their position of power and rank, with who would be seated on the right hand in the afterlife than with the lessons Jesus was teaching them.

[211] Brougeault, *Wisdom Jesus*, 186-9.

power is unitive – not divisive. Everything Jesus taught was antithetical to the power concepts of his time and of the power concepts most societies still hold onto today. To be in Christ means that we must accept the offer Jesus made – to be food for his friends and to be consumed in the process. On the heels of that, "Jesus said to his disciples, 'It is good that I am leaving you.' Otherwise, Panikkar writes, 'we would make him king — that is, an idol — or we would rigidify him into concepts, into intellectual containers. We would turn his teaching into a system, imprison him within our own categories and suffocate the Spirit.' Rather, Jesus knew that it was good that he leave, that he had not come to remain but to remain in us in the most perfect form, not as a more or less welcome guest foreign to us but in our very being. This is the meaning of the Eucharist."[212] Nonetheless, church and society took all of his messages and venerated them and him as symbols of power, glory and worship instead of practices (that are quite difficult) to be followed. In the end, Christianity must be a practice, not a religion.

Ontology and Eschatology

One could argue that all theology is a system of meaning-making. It stems from the innate human wondering why: Why do we feel that presence? Why are we here, in this place? Why do we feel love and loved? It is a theology of origins. How did we get this way? Where did it all begin? How do we explain the origin of the world, the cosmos, and of humans as they exist today? Our ancestors had only their own experience on which they could draw. So of course they made up a world that centered on them, their existence and their world (though they thought it to be their cosmos, we now know it to be only a tiny sliver of the entire reality). The creation myth, the story of original man (Adam) and original woman (Eve) and the fall from grace helped our ancestors make sense of our broken nature and our tendency toward narcissistic error. There had to be a reason, so they created one. All peoples do – we crave meaning.

So from that time we have developed systems of thought based on our original sin, on our nature as a fallen people, who (must have) once lived in grace and who, through our wonton ways, got expelled from that garden. However what was forgotten in the mythos, the story-telling, was that the "original sin" that was storied to be the source of our fallen nature was the dualistic desire to know and name all things as either good or evil. Thus ontological systematics (that is a systematic theology based on the nature of things as the source of meaning structures) builds a structure that copes with our fallen nature and provides a process for reinstatement into grace, to wit, the incarnation of God in Jesus, the

---

[212] Delio, *Christ in Evolution*, Kindle Locations 1810-1814.

avatar of God (as Harvard theologian, Gordon Kaufman, calls it[213]) and savior of God's people. However, Jesus never taught that we needed to be saved. Rather he claimed that we were already not simply saved, we were chosen heirs to the kingdom. In other words Jesus did not have to die for our sins – our sins were already/always forgiven – before we even asked. The parable of the prodigal son tells us that! Why then, we ask, did Jesus have to die? Because dying was the only way to show the immensity of God's sustaining love. Dying was the way of pure self-emptying. It was only in actually dying and returning that we humans could possibly see the truth that love is found on the other side of the death of self/ego.

John of the Cross, though steeped in a world of systematics that not only deified Jesus, but further deified Mary, his mother, and made saints out of humans who lived the pure and ascetic life, turned his back on all that structure and focused instead on the simple experience of loving and being loved by God. It was not so much a rejection of the theology of the times, but rather his seeing no need for the superstructure of theological discourse. God was personal and palpable to John of the Cross. In casting off his sandals[214] John was saying that true theology was a simple experience, a naked experience, and one that is focused on the experience of living into that feeling (rather than trying to "pontificate" on its meaning).

Loving on the human plane is a perfect analogy for the love we experience through and from God. In order to become fully known by another person we must fully risk our whole being, becoming vulnerable by fully losing ourselves in loving the other. In the same way the infinite divine risked everything in the incarnation to become known by us. If we take the words of John 3:16 to heart in this context, it reads: that God "so loved" God's creatures that God entered into and experienced love as another human so that we might know that love and experience the infinite (everlasting life) in that encounter.

What was missing in my early seminary theology and had yet to be discovered in my journey through the dark nights was that both the beginning and the end are included in the present. Life is only available in the present moment. Love is only present in the moment of now. All else is fantasy or vanity, says the proverb. If love is God and God is love, both are only available in the present moment, which is why the theology of the dark night reduces to a theology of praxis: getting one's mind to stay in the present moment is – by virtue of the

---

[213] Gordon Kaufman,, *In Face of Mystery: A Constructive Theology*, (Cambridge, MA: Harvard University Press, 1993), 397.

[214] John had joined Teresa of Avila's order of "Discalced" (meaning Shoeless) Carmelites, whose main thrust was to experience life in the purest and simplest form – without all the trappings of mainline theology. He ultimately became their chief confessor and spiritual director.

human mind itself – nearly impossible. We can go there, we can create practices to take us into the present, but no sooner do we experience that moment of presence (and therefore experience God/love/the infinite), than we slip into awareness of the self's need to wonder how it got there or where this is all going (if we give credit to our higher being) or maybe just what's for dinner (which is more like my mundane conscious mind). So our connection in intimacy comes and goes, and our practices must be those practices that return us to the simple present moment. It is only in the act of self-emptying love and self-emptying giving that we become fully present and it is precisely for that reason that the teachings of mystics like John of the Cross utilized both contemplation (kenosis) and action (praxis) as the major tools for getting to God.

In contemplation, intimacy with God becomes as common as breathing. But like in breathing, we need to remember that while half of the time we are inhaling – breathing in the breath of God – the other half we exhale. And sometimes that exhaling is in exasperation forgetting that the next breath brings us back in oneness with the Almighty. The dark night of the soul, at some point, becomes a regular occurrence – an awareness of the dance of presence and absence. We cannot know absence (the void of feeling apart from God) unless and until we first know presence (being a part of God, loved by God). Life for me – my spiritual life – has become an exploration of that world; seeking the boundary of absence/presence. And the strange and unnerving awareness I have come to is that the absence/presence line is on the border of unconscious and conscious knowing. That which I know – the world of my thoughts, awareness, words, and concepts – is the place where I am most estranged from that presence and where my experience is of the absence of God. And those places wherein I am most mindless, most ego-less, most in service to another, most humbled (or humiliated as I like to refer to it) by my lack of understanding, are the places most filled with the presence of God and the presence of love. The so-called dark places are no longer dark and foreboding; they are reminders that I have turned away from the light and into my own petty world of "knowing." I am exhaling – putting out just so much air (though to me it seems as though I must be speaking and uttering intelligent sounds of some sort), and it is time again to shut up, and listen – inhale the present, the presence of love.

If I were to make any overarching generalizations about the data I have collected thus far, it would be that the dark night of the soul is not just part and parcel of the spiritual journey, it may be the primary force at work in our spiritual development. In a postmodern world, rife with technological advances that simultaneously remove us from personal contact and yet remove the barriers of intimacy wherein any part of our previously private lives are now accessible to nearly anyone else out there, pastors dealing with the spiritual well-being of their parishioners, must be prepared to guide those spiritual journeys into new and different territories than ministers have ever encountered before. It may be that, as Constance FitzGerald contends, we are entering into a dark night of the church's soul. All of those organized religious structures, systems, credos and mythical story lines have fallen into meaninglessness and the very fabric of the church's "one foundation" is called into question and as a result believers, and the congregation as a whole is thrust into the dark night.

The meaninglessness of traditional theologies fall too quickly to be able to sustain any of the seekers' needs. Ministers and pastors of all kinds must be conversant in the mysteries of the dark night. We must know its centrality to the faith journey. Not only is it central to the faith journey (and the overwhelming majority of ministers responding to my survey concur with me), it is the power that refines and strengthens one's faith. We must become more conversant in the language of the night.

The Nightlife of the Soul[215]

The daytime hours are ruled by the conscious mind and thus by ego and self. We all have our day jobs to do, whether, as in the case of the ministers surveyed, that work is pastoral, or in my case or so many others, simply doing the job we have chosen as our vocation. But in the night (both temporal night and the night of the soul), in our dreams and our most quiet hours, the soul lives and plays out its themes. No longer does this send a chill up my spine like it used to. I have had times when I resisted sleep for fear of the monsters that might rise up and take hold of me in the dark. That was before I was introduced to the darkness of the night of the soul. But now I see that time as sacred. I even use my meditation time to extend and expand the nightlife of my soul. By this, I am not claiming that every night is another excursion into the dark night of the soul, nor that every night is spent working through the bigger issues of life. Rather, I am referring here to those times when our nighttime is spent working through, dealing with and processing our bigger and more spiritual issues.

In the nightlife of the soul there is much work to be done – it's not exactly a party scene. To be certain it is the time when dreams work at playing out the themes and choices of life's daytime world. But more importantly it is a time of fallow, or resting in trust and faith enough to replenish and refuel the life force within, and to meet up with God, face to face, as it were. Clearly part of the nightlife of the soul is cleansing – bathing in the love of God. While at times that bathing may feel more like the sintering crucible, or to use John of the Cross's

---

[215] Thanks to Barbara Brown Taylor for the metaphor of the nightlife of the soul. Though it appears as a chapter heading in her book, *Learning to Walk in the Dark*, (New York: HarperOne, 2014), I have borrowed it and will be using it in a slightly different way, describing the mechanics of what happens in the night.

metaphor like a log burning in the fire, bathing in love is the place where the pollution of one's ego is washed away and the soul is hung out to dry.

But in more specific language, the nightlife of the soul is where SELF is developed devoid of little self's petty concerns and worries. Whether God actively leads a believer into the dark night or not (i.e., is this an active night or passive night of the soul?) is immaterial. The point of the dark night is that in the presence of unconditional love, pettiness and self-seeking cannot survive. Just as cancer cannot survive in an oxygen rich environment, egoism cannot survive when bathed in unconditional and infinite love. In the night, the soul stops resisting all else and lets everything in.

In the daylight hours we try our best to cope with situations and the curve-balls life throws at us. But in the night of the soul, we learn that everything serves the greater agenda. Please do not hear that as any sort of predestination or predetermination belief. Life events do not happen "for a reason." Life simply happens. It is how we react to those life events that makes all the difference. Can we trust in the unconditional and unending love of God to sustain us? Can we have the faith that Jesus always praised as the healing process? Or will we succumb to our petty egoic whine of "why me?" Gerald May, who was intimately familiar with John of the Cross and the mystics, wrote the following insight in his journal, *The Wisdom of Wilderness* shortly before he passed away:

> In my psychiatric practice how many times did I help patients cope with their feelings, tame the power of their emotions? I no longer believe that was helpful. Even when I assisted people in uncovering long-buried emotions, I seldom encouraged them to savor the life-juice of the feelings themselves: the rich dark love nature of grief, the warming fire of anger, the subtle luminosity of loneliness, the gut-driving power of sexual desire, or the exquisite clarity of fear.
>
> Instead, for the most part, I helped them cope. I have come to hate that word, because to cope with something you have to separate yourself from it. You make it your antagonist, your enemy. Like management, coping is a taming word, sometimes even a warfare word. Wild, untamed emotions are full of life-spirit, vibrant with the energy of being. They don't have to be acted out, but neither do they need to be tamed. They are part of our inner wilderness; they can just be what they are. God save me from coping. God help me join, not separate. Help me be with and in, not apart

from. Show me the way to savoring, not controlling. Dear God, hear my prayer: make me forever copeless.[216]

And after a time, the soul actually seeks the dark. It can't wait for the lights to go out, whether subtly through centering prayer and meditation, at the end of the working day when the ego takes off it suit and hangs up its boxing gloves, or as May did, on long walks in the wilderness. The soul seeks the night because it is there that the soul, the SELF, comes alive, builds it strength and takes over by welcoming the dark, welcoming the uncomfortable, welcoming the disquieting and ego-disturbing elements of life.

The nightlife of the soul is not a frolicking all-night party. It is a feet-on-the-ground clarity of seeing things for what they really are, devoid of any attempt to see how they might serve the ego or self. It is a time of fluid giving and receiving that flows as easily as inhaling and exhaling. It is a time of resting in God, having found that God was here, in the innermost part of one's being all along. It is a time of smiling knowingly at all the effort one has spent in digging and searching for what one perceived as illusive and finding it, at last, right there on the very ground from which one started searching.

In Conclusion

The inherited religion with which we grew up has been exposed as a static model based on a static geocentric and anthropocentric cosmology that no longer holds water. Modern biblical scholarship now holds that "stories of the Old and New Testaments were prayerfully created for the purpose of community, rather than as historical narratives."[217] If we cling to an outmoded static conception of a God who rules this static universe we are faced with an inescapable dissonance of constructs that rattles us to the core. It is no wonder that postmodern ministers face a crisis of faith. They do not need a Newtown Connecticut to trigger their dark night – it is inevitable from living into this world while attempting to force-fit a 16th century religion into it! Religious life just cannot fit into it. And as I often quip to my atheistic friend, "The God you don't believe in, I do not believe in either!" Living a spiritual life and walking a spiritual path calls the question: how will you resolve the unmistakable feeling of presence with the death of a static conceptual God slain by the "truths" of modern science?

---

[216] Gerald May, *The Wisdom of Wilderness, Experiencing the Healing Power of Nature* (New York: HarperCollins e-books, 2007), 34 (Kindle location 58).

[217] Ilia Delio, *The Unbearable Wholeness of Being: God, Evolution, and the Power of Love* (Orbis Books: Kindle Edition, 2013), Kindle locations 134-135.

Modern science has opened our eyes to a dynamic world of continual change, of fractals and chaos theories that reach into the furthest dimensions of the cosmos. If religion is to stay alive, and resume its appointed role of helping individuals make sense of their world and their role within the cosmos, then it must adopt a theological stance that incorporates and embraces the principles of science and evolution. Teilhard's contention was that Christ must be born again. Christ must be reincarnated in a world that has become too different from that in which Jesus lived. To which Delio adds, "I believe that the Messiah whom we await, whom we all without any doubt await, is the universal Christ; that is to say, the Christ of evolution."[218] That Christ, the Christ of love becoming incarnate as the unfolding universe, is the beingness of and manifestation of love, i.e., of God.

Astronomers today have been questioning the big bang. How did it occur and what were the events leading up to it that caused such an incredible explosion that resulted in the creation of the expanding universe that we see today? One of their hypotheses seems to be that matter collapsed in on itself creating an unthinkable density so immense that it could collapse no further and at that point it exploded, sending into play a chains of events and reactions that formed stars and galaxies hurtling off into the furthest reaches of space.

But they also speculate that the expansion seems to be slowing and that at some point, this expanding will exceed the thrust of the initial big bang explosion and the gravity of all those countless stars and galaxies will begin to pull them all back toward each other, such that in another billion trillion years the whole thing will collapse in on itself once again. And then, (you guessed it) another explosion. Over and over, again and again, across the unthinkable stretches of time, the cosmos will expand and contract, and expand and contract.

Like a gigantic,

cosmic,

beating

heart.

What if the nature of the universe, the nature of the entire cosmos, were a beating heart? What if the nature of all creation was a heart; was love, beating out a rhythm of love that was the source of all creation? Could this be what we want to name God? Could God be the entire heartbeat of all creation? When we lose the anthropocentric worldview and subsequently, the heliocentric view of a God exclusive to this solar system and this world; when we contemplate that God is the essence, source and totality of the cosmos, our understanding of incarnation takes on new meaning. Ilia Delio, who speaks of Christ as the incarnation, writes:

---

[218] Delio, *Christ in Evolution,* Kindle Locations 2603-2605.

John Haught has spoken of evolution as Darwin's gift to theology, and I think we can say here that evolution is, in particular, Darwin's gift to Christology. For the whole concept of evolution has liberated Christ from the limits of the man Jesus and enabled us to locate Christ at the heart of creation: the primacy of God's love, the exemplar of creation, the centrating principle of evolution, and the Omega point of an evolutionary universe. Rather than fixing our attention on a lonely, static figure of Jesus Christ, we can now locate Christ at the heart of the whole evolutionary process: from cosmic evolution to biological evolution to evolution of human consciousness and culture.[219]

God is love. I am love. And "love is the fundamental energy of evolution."[220] I am in God and God is in me, and you, and all else in creation. All creation is one united being in the process of becoming that full expression of love – the force which draws all things toward each other in unity. When John of the Cross got to that point of clarity, it was no wonder why, in pure ecstasy, he wrote the poem *The Dark Night of the Soul*. Clearly he had seen the face of God and was transformed by the light that shines in the darkness.

On a dark night,
Kindled in love with yearnings–oh, happy chance!–
I went forth without being observed,
My house being now at rest.

In darkness and secure,
By the secret ladder, disguised–oh, happy chance!–
In darkness and in concealment,
My house being now at rest.

In the happy night,
In secret, when none saw me,
Nor I beheld aught,
Without light or guide, save that which burned in my heart.

This light guided me
More surely than the light of noonday

---

[219] Delio, *Christ in Evolution*, Kindle locations 3201-3206.

[220] Delio, *The Unbearable Wholeness*, Kindle locations 287-288.

To the place where he (well I knew who!) was awaiting me–
A place where none appeared.

Oh, night that guided me,
Oh, night more lovely than the dawn,
Oh, night that joined Beloved with lover,
Lover transformed in the Beloved!

Upon my flowery breast,
Kept wholly for himself alone,
There he stayed sleeping, and I caressed him,
And the fanning of the cedars made a breeze.

The breeze blew from the turret
As I parted his locks;
With his gentle hand he wounded my neck
And caused all my senses to be suspended.

I remained, lost in oblivion;
My face I reclined on the Beloved.
All ceased and I abandoned myself,
Leaving my cares forgotten among the lilies.[221]

I began this thesis hoping to find a way to give assistance to those going through the dark night and perhaps to guide those who would help them in their pain and darkness. It had been my contention that the study of theology moved a spiritual person into a headier, more theoretical place, when in fact what may have motivated a seeker to pursue a career in theology was a mystical experience (that is, a personal experience of the spiritual). But when religion becomes mere ideology it moves away from a trust in the personal and mystical. On the inward journey, in the dark night of the soul, when spirit burns away the false self, one's soul is able to live in mystery and the fullness of now.

In my research I met and spoke with people whose lives were changed by the dark night, whose compassion for others was awakened by their own pain and suffering, and whose experience of being unconditionally loved had transformed them and their theological "certainties." But the wisdom of the night is that there

[221] John of the Cross, *Dark Night*, 1-2.

is no other way. Rohr says that the only things that have the power to transform us are extreme suffering and unconditional love.[222] In the darkness of this night both collide in a glorious way that one would be foolish to deny any person. It is the same collision of love and suffering that is most visible in the crucifixion. The dark night of the soul is an invitation to the intersection of suffering and love, an invitation to the crucifixion of self/ego, literally to follow Jesus to the crucifixion. In our fullest compassion perhaps the best we can do for and with another going through this night, is to love them and hold them in our compassion.

The stories of the dark night are sacred texts written in the hearts and souls of those who bravely stepped into the darkness (or those who had no other choice and were thrust on to this path). And we who have traveled with them, and have witnessed with them, or have been in that dark forest ourselves have heard a story of faith, of hope and of infinite love. Cardinal Newman once said, "So much holiness is lost to the world because Christians do not share the secrets of their hearts one with another."[223] Perhaps these secrets of the heart as one passes through the dark night of the soul need to be shared, or need to be given a place of light where others can learn from them and take comfort in them. Perhaps we need to become, like Theresa, saints of darkness, lighting the way for those in the dark night. But given the sacredness of this journey, perhaps our best practice should be simply to hang out a "do not disturb" sign.

Let it be.

---

[222] Rohr, *Job*, 105.
[223] As related in discussion with Fr. Richard Rohr September 2014.

Afterword – Learning to Walk in the Dark

Afterword: Learning to Walk in the Dark

> The dark night of the soul is a journey into the light, a journey
> from your darkness into the strength and hidden resources of your
> soul. Navigating the dark night requires interior dialogue,
> contemplation, prayer, quiet time and sharing with those who
> understand the profound nature of inner transformation. When you
> are in this interior place, you stand at the crossroads of your
> power, between your ego and your soul, between time and
> timelessness.
>
> Caroline Myss

This thesis was begun in an effort to open the discussion of the dark night
of the soul. While it is clear from this investigation that a great number of
ordained ministers do encounter their own crises of faith and feel that they have
endured a "dark night of the soul," it is equally clear that a crisis of spirituality is
not limited to those in the profession. If I may be so bold, I would wager that the
dark night is a necessary part of the spiritual journey, like a reptile shedding its
skin in order to grow larger. Our simplistic beliefs must die and be shed for the
new experiences and encounters of the divine to come in. However,
"unfortunately" (or perhaps it is fortune disguised as unfortunate), this forms the
new skin as our ego wrestles it to the ground in an effort to lay claim to
"knowing" it. All too soon that skin gets stiff and confining to the spiritual seeker
and once again, must be shed.

We live in a time when we think we have a right as humans to experience
life without pain or pressure, without setbacks or sorrows. We medicate even the
slightest pain or angst. Pharmaceuticals, and in particular antidepressants are the
largest selling products in the world with estimated annual sales in the trillions.
But the myth that all pain is bad or worse yet, the spiritual belief that God should
not allow us (good people) to have to endure pain and suffering is childish and
debilitating. Ministers are continually asked "why" and "how could such a thing
happen?" to which they have no scriptural response – because that is not how life
is and that is not who/what God is. There is no rescuer-God in the Bible. God
never saved Job; God's presence sat with Joseph and Paul in the stench of their
prison terms, and was the reality that Jesus and Stephen and so many others "saw"
in the darkest moments of their pain and dying, but "God" did not stop the
process.

While writing this paper three events happened that, had I not been engaged in "Wrestling the Angel," I might have experienced differently: my business suffered a major setback and eventually had to be closed (at a significant emotional loss and an even bigger financial loss); a close friend, a man on my men's team, discovered suddenly that he had stage four, metastasized cancer; and in the middle of dealing with that, my best friend– a man with whom I spoke, without exception, every Thursday morning – 5:30 promptly – for the last 15 years since he had moved to Florida – died suddenly of a massive brain hemorrhage. Instead of wondering what in the world was happening, I prayed more – not the "Dear God take this away" prayer one might be tempted to scream out, but the calm centering prayer that just sits in silence and waits for the ego to shut up and make way for divine love to re-enter. And here is what I saw.

I was at first amazed at what my teammate, James, was saying during his last months and weeks in the hospital. His cancer placed him squarely in the face of his mortality and catapulted his spirituality to a state far beyond where he had been, as well as beyond his current operating stage. His compassion for others and disregard for himself showed a level of advanced spirituality I had rarely encountered. I would go to the hospital during his chemo treatments just to listen to him retell the visions he had been having – visions of being in the presence of the divine and of beings made of light – and discuss how this dark night had peeled away layers and layers of his ego. Like the Biblical transformations I mentioned previously, he actually had a different name for each of his previous egoic manifestations (Jim, then James, and then Matthew) so he could differentiate them and how they each held different conceptualizations of the divine. He was, in my opinion, now speaking from a unitive consciousness that seemed almost free of ego. He was clearly standing in the light. In a way his encounters with death and mortality prepared me for death of my business and the sudden death of my friend.

My best friend, Peter, had a worn out heart but he qualified for a transplant. He had been waiting for some months before being transferred to Los Angeles where his chances were better for finding a match. But the window of opportunity was closing rapidly, so they outfitted him with an artificial heart. On one call I noticed how angry he was – cursing like a sailor! This man, who I knew as one of the most caring and giving men in my life, was so filled with what sounded like rage until he explained, "I have no heart; I'm the fucking Tin Man! I'm not angry at anyone else, it's that without a heart all this unresolved anger is coming up inside of me."

Then some young soul died and a heart became available (I have to acknowledge that loss of life which made it possible) and they prepared Peter for surgery. But at the last minute it was determined to not be a match. Our exhilaration quickly crashed. Then, miraculously, less than a day later there was another life given up and this heart was a perfect match. Peter went into surgery on a Friday night and the text from his wife Saturday morning was that it was a success. The heart was beating strongly inside of him and he was smiling and awake. And then, just as suddenly, 12 hours later his head exploded with a massive brain hemorrhage, and he was gone. He died like he lived; in giving, and they kept his body going until all his usable parts were donated. When his wife called me to let me know what had happened his body was still living.

A few weeks later, I flew to Florida for what I was told would be a memorial service to "say a few words" about my friend. But when I arrived, I was crushed by the grief of his wife and six year old daughter. I had written some stupidly funny things we had shared, great times that would be wonderful remembrances of this great man. But on entering that space, I realized this was a funeral, a time for the grieving that no one had yet done – not a "memorial" tribute to a great man.

So I ripped up my notes and spoke what was in my heart. I spoke as a fellow traveler through the dark night. Though I don't remember exactly the extemporaneous words, I said something like this: "Though Peter and I loved to disagree on many things," I said, "the one thing we agreed on was that God is love – not God is loving like some giant father in the sky that cradles his children – but that God IS love itself. And we also agreed that God is eternal, which therefore means that love is eternal and enduring. Love does not end when a friend moves to Florida, nor does it end when he ceases to live in this form. I love Peter. You love Peter – that is why we are here today. But that love does not stop here or a few Sundays ago when he passed on.

"Love never dies, because love is the divine, the eternal element in each one of us. Pain, sorrow, horrific events – that all happens because the world is just a chaotic place. But love – that which gives us life – love is eternal. The lesson we learn in grief, in the dark nights of our soul's despairing, is that love creeps in and sidles up next to us, and wraps us up, and just rocks us gently until the tears stop and the pain subsides.

"Deeply loving someone who loved us so deeply is the model Jesus gave us. But it leaves us wondering what to do with all this love – because, as Paul said, 'Love never stops.' He went on to say, 'Love bears all things, hopes all things and endures all things.' So let your faith be strong, let you heart hope for the time when this hurts a little less, but remember always to love. In loving we keep Peter in our hearts; in loving, we reflect the perfect love of God, and in loving we comfort each other. When everything else we desire is taken away, we still have and we always will have love."

Oh, by the way, there was a young minister there who opportunistically used his brief homily to spew some platitudes about how Jesus would walk with them and take away all their sorrow, and to ask people to raise their hand if they wanted to accept Jesus, right then, as their personal savior, and he would come and talk to them after the service (we were to have our eyes closed, but I peeked – there were no hands up). I couldn't tell if I felt sorry for him or sorry for myself that I no longer had that simple belief in a God who would take it all away for me. We all just felt hurt, and that was what we were supposed to feel! We did not need nor want a Prozac Jesus.

Later that fall, I faced a third loss and had to close my business. It wasn't just a business, though. It was an early childhood education center filled with a hundred little ones from neonates to five years of age. It was a wonderful job and I fell in love with 100 infants and toddlers multiple times a day. But the problem was that we could not stabilize the teaching staff and that lack of stability is not healthy for little children. So ultimately the decision came down to cutting way back to just two classrooms (which translated into a kind of Sophie's choice of who we sent away), or closing entirely. We felt it best to do the latter.

I wanted to make sure each child was placed in another school so I invited the owners and directors of all our competitors to come in our last week and help us find placements. Tuesday night of that last week I was in my office late, copying all the children's files to help in the outplacement. There, in the darkness, surrounded by stacks of yellow files, it suddenly hit me that these were not pieces of paper – these were children; children I loved and had sworn to protect, children who looked up at my six foot frame with those innocent eyes, and trusted me.

And I started to cry. It was a convulsive, deep wailing cry. And I could not stop. I cried all the way home, and ran into my bedroom and buried my head in the pillows, and I just screamed. I cried for the children. I cried for Peter. I cried for James. I mourned all those losses and felt the pain, and I felt so very small and insignificant.

It was the dark night of the soul.

As I said at the outset of this chapter, had I not studied this and talked to so many others who had been through it, and had I not had excursions into the dark night before, I may have lost reality this time. And at the same time I am well aware that the more ideas one has about how the dark operates the more one is blinded to what is really happening – I had to let it happen. I had no choice. Whichever was the case, after four hours of convulsive sobbing, I fell asleep. And the next day when I awoke, something was different. I was empty. But the difference this time was that it felt as though the inside of me had not just been emptied out but that the whole container had been washed clean. I was not able to put any of it into words and I spoke to no one at first. But gradually I started to be able to talk.

I was fortunate to have been in a spiritual program called "The Living School" and under the tutelage of Richard Rohr, Cynthia Bourgeault and Jim Finley – and (strangely) coincidently, two weeks after that night I flew to Albuquerque for our final symposium. Cynthia, Jim and Richard, their assistant staff and my peers were the net into which my free fall landed. And because they knew the ways of the dark night, they knew how to just listen, to let me fall, and to accept all of what I needed to process.

But others may not have the fortune of a spiritual director or a safety net as large as the one I had. And this begs the question of how we prepare others for this journey. How will we be able to support others on whom the dark night comes to call?

The church of the 21st century is in spiritual and theological crisis. There are some who might claim that this is the church's dark night of the soul.[224] Our country is divided into fundamentalists who want a quick fix and a theology of right and wrong duality, and a mass of others reeling in a post-election apocalypse they fear will set social services and efforts for justice back a hundred years. On a theological level, no longer do the routines and rituals of a post renaissance theology satisfy the hunger of persons who seek meaning in their lives. Millennials want substance not platitudes and reality in place of rehashed aphorisms.

The dark night of the soul – the dark night of the church's soul – may become more of our regular collective experience than the closeted tribulations of a select few. Our churches and our social organizations may all be in crisis like the dark night of the soul. We are faced with hard questions and have far too few satisfactory solutions. In the dark night, that which meaningless falls away and that which is supports the egoic need for self or future certainty falls into nothingness. What one discovers in the darkness is a raw reality that transcends words, platitudes or aphorisms. What one discovers in the darkness is that spirituality is a process of discovery; that what is known, was known or can be expressed in simple terms is surely not of the essence of the spirit.

Barbara Brown Taylor puts it very well when she writes:

---

[224] Constance FitzGerald, "From Impasse to Prophetic Hope: Crisis of Memory." *CTSA Proceedings*, (Catholic Theological Society of America), 64 (2009), 41.

Once you have emerged from whatever safe religious place you have been in, recognizing that your view of the world is one worldview among many, discovering the historical Jesus, revolutionizing your understanding of scripture, and updating your theology, once you have changed the way you do church, or at least change the music at your church and hired a pastor who tweets, or you can no longer find any church within a 50 mile radius in which you can let down your guard long enough to pray, once the Dalai Lama starts making as much sense to you as the Pope or your favorite preacher and your rare but renovating encounters with the Divine reduce all your best words to dust, well, what's left for you to hold onto? After so many years of trying to cobble together a way of thinking about God that makes sense so that I can safely settle down with it, it all turns to *nada*. There is no permanently safe place to settle. I will always be at sea, steering by the stars. Yet as dark as this sounds, it provides great relief, because it now sounds truer than any thing that came before.[225]

The dark night is a place of healing and transformation. It is not something "to get better" from, like getting over a bout of depression. When depression passes, your life is somewhat restored to what it was but when the dark night passes, you have been transformed, and nothing is the same. Safety – or at least the safety net – has been taken away. As Meister Eckhart wrote, "the soul grows by subtraction, not addition."

Perhaps the future of the church rests in our collective ability to let go of our "understanding" and learn to free-fall into the abyss of love that is the true presence of God. It is a course that is largely uncharted and certainly not something that can be layered into a hierarchical system of an organized structure like traditional churches have been. Perhaps it is only something that can be lived and shared; one person at a time and, as I have said, one moment at a time. My prayer is that this work that I have presented here may in some way help to open doors to that discussion.

---

[225] Taylor, *Learning to Walk*, 139-140.

Works Cited

Ackerman, John. *Listening to God*. Minneapolis: Alban Institute, 2001.

Armstrong, Karen. *The Great Transformation*. New York: Alfred Knopf, 2006.

_____. *The Spiral Staircase*. New York: Anchor Books, 2004.

Auden, W. H. *For the Time Being: A Christmas Oratorio*. Princeton: Princeton University Press, 2013. http://www.cs.utsa.edu/~wagner/church/auden/ on 10/6/13.

Benefiel, Margaret. *Soul at Work*. Seabury: New York, 2005.

_____. *The Soul of a Leader*. New York: Crossroads Publishing Co., 2008.

Benner, David. *Spirituality and the Awakening Self: the Sacred Journey of Transformation*. Grand Rapids: Brazos Press, 2012.

Bolman, Lee and Terrence Deal. *Leading with Soul*. San Francisco: Jossey-Bass, 1995.

Bondi, Roberta. *To Love as God Loves: Conversations With the Early Church*. Philadelphia: Fortress Press, 1987.

Bourgeault, Cynthia, *The Wisdom Jesus, Transforming Heart and Mind – A New Perspective on Christ and His Message*, Boston: Shambala, 2008.

Bragdon, Emma. *The Call of Spiritual Emergency: From Pastoral Crisis to Personal Transformation*. Woodstock, VT: eBookIt.com, 2013.

Bringle, Mary Louise. *Despair: Sickness or Sin?* Nashville, TN: Abingdon Press, 1990.

Brueggemann, Walter. *Hopeful Imagination: Prophetic Voices in Exile*. Philadelphia: Fortress Press, 1986.

Buckley, Michael J. "Atheism and Contemplation." Unpublished paper for the Jesuit School of Theology in Berkeley, accessed February 20, 2014 http://www.ts.mu.edu/readers/content/pdf/40/40.4/40.4.2.pdf

Campbell, Joseph. *Thou Art That*. Novato, CA: New World Library, 2001.

Chodron, Pema. *When Things Fall Apart, Heart Advice for Difficult Times*. Boston: Shambhala, 2002.

Coe, J. "Musing on the dark night of the soul: Insights from St. John of the Cross on a developmental spirituality." *Journal of Psychology and Theology*, Winter, 2000.

Delio, Ilia. *Christ in Evolution*. Maryknoll, NY: Orbis Books, 2008.

_____. *The Unbearable Wholeness of Being: God, Evolution, and the Power of Love*. Orbis Books: Kindle Edition, 2013.

Elrod, P. David and Donald Tippett. "The 'Death Valley' of Change." *Journal of Organizational Change Management*, 2002, 15:3.

Finley, James. *The Divine Ambush*, lecture delivered for The Center for Action and Contemplation, Santa Fe, NM, April 18-20, 2013.

Finley, James, *Merton's Palace of Nowhere*, Notre Dame, IN: Notre Dame Press, 1978.

FitzGerald, Constance. "Impasse and Dark Night," in *Living with Apocalypse, Spiritual resources for Social Compassion*. Tilden Edwards, ed., San Francisco: HarperCollins, 1984, pp. 93-116.

_____. "From Impasse to Prophetic Hope: Crisis of Memory." *CTSA Proceedings*, (Catholic Theological Society of America), 64 (2009), 21-42.

Fowler, James, *Stages of Faith: The Psychology of Human Faith and the Quest for Meaning,* New York, HarperCollins, 1978

Greun, Anselm, *Heaven Begins Within You*, New York, Crossroads Publishing Co., 2011

Grof, Stanislas and Christina Grof. *Spiritual Emergency: When Personal Transformation Becomes a Crisis.* New York: Penguin, 1989.

Gutierrez, Gustavo. *On Job, God Talk and the Suffering of the Innocent.* Translated by Matthew J. O'Connell. Maryknoll, NY: Orbis Books, 1987.

Heifetz, Ronald. *Leadership Without Easy Answers*. Cambridge, MA: Belknap Press, Harvard University, 1994.

Heifetz, Ronald and Marty Linsky. *Leadership on the Line, Staying Alive Through the Dangers of Leading*. Boston: Harvard Business School Publishing, 2002.

Holmes, Barbara. *Joy Unspeakable, Contemplative Practices of the Black Church*. Minneapolis, MN: Augsburg Press, 2004.

Howells, Edward and Peter Tyler, eds. Sources of Transformation: Revitalising Christian Spirituality. London: Continuum International Publishing Group, 2010.

Johnston William. *Mystical Theology: The Science of Love*. Maryknoll, NY: Orbis Books, 1996.

Kahane, Adam. *Solving Tough Problems, An Open Way of Talking, Listening and Creating New Realities*. San Francisco: Berrett-Koehler Publications, 2004.

Kaufman, Gordon. In Face of Mystery: A Constructive Theology. Cambridge, MA: Harvard University Press, 1993.

Kidd, Sue Monk. *When the Heart Waits: Spiritual Direction for Life's Sacred Questions*. New York: HarperCollins, 1990.

Kleiger, James H. "Emerging from the 'dark night of the soul:' Healing the false self in a narcissistically vulnerable minister." *Psychoanalytic Psychology*, Vol. 7(2), 1990, 211-224.

Kolodiejchuk, Brian. *Mother Teresa: Come Be My Light*. New York: Doubleday, 2007.

Kubler-Ross, Elisabeth. *On Death and Dying*. New York: Schribner, 1969.

Kushner, Harold. *The Book of Job, When Bad Things Happen To A Good Person*. New York: Schocken Books/Random House, 2012.

Lewis, Thomas, Fari Amini, and Richard Lannon. *A General Theory of Love*. New York: Vintage Books, 2000.

Libanio, JB. *Spiritual Discernment and Politics: Guidelines for Religious Communities*. Maryknoll, NY: Orbis Books, 1977.

Loder, James. *The Transforming Moment*. Colorado Springs: Helmers and Howard, 1989.

_____. *The Logic of the Spirit: Human Development in Theological Perspective*. San Francisco: Jossey-Bass, 1998.

Love, Patrick. "Comparing Spiritual Development and Cognitive Development." *Journal of College Student Development*, May 2002.

May, Gerald. *The Dark Night of the Soul*. San Francisco: HarperCollins Publishers, 2004.

_____. *The Wisdom of Wilderness, Experiencing the Healing Power of Nature*. New York: HarperCollins e-books, 2007.

McCall, Morgan, Mike Lombardo & Ann Morrison. *The Lessons of Experience*. New York: Free Press/Simon and Schuster, 1988.

Meadow, Mary Jo. "The Dark side of Mysticism: Depression and the 'Dark Night.'" *Pastoral Psychology*, Vol. 33(2), Winter 1984.

Merton, Thomas. *The Wisdom of the Desert*. New York: Abbey of Gethsemane, New Directions Press, 1960.

_____. *New Seeds of Contemplation*. New York: New Directions Books, 1961.

Missler, Nancy. *Faith in the Night Seasons*. Coeur d'Alene, ID: King's High Way Ministries, Inc., 2012.

Moore, Thomas. *Dark Nights of the Soul, A guide to Finding Your Way Through Life's Ordeals*. New York: Gotham Books, 2004.

Myss, Carolyn. *Spiritual Madness*. Sounds True Recordings, 2002.

Perry, William G., Jr. "Cognitive and Ethical Growth: The Making of Meaning." In A. W. Chickering & Assoc. (Eds.), *The Modern American College*. (pp. 76-116). San Francisco: Jossey-Bass, 1981.

Quinn, Robert. *Deep Change, Discovering the Leader Within.* San Francisco: Jossey-Bass, 1996.

Rilke, Rainer Maria. "The Man Watching." Accessed March 22, 2008, from http://www.cdra.org.za/creativity/Rainer%20Maria%20Rilke%20-%20The%20Man%20Watching.htm.

Rizzuto, Ana-Maria. *The Battle for the Living God.* Chicago: University of Chicago Press, 1981.

Rohr, Richard. *Adam's Return.* New York: Crossroads Publishing, 2004.

_____. *Everything Belongs: The Gift of Contemplative Prayer.* New York: Crossroad Publications, 2003.

_____. *Things Hidden.* Cincinnati, OH: Saint Anthony Messenger Press, 2008.

_____. *The Naked Now.* New York: Crossroads Publishing Co., 2009.

_____. *Breathing Under Water.* Cincinnati, OH: St. Anthony Messenger Press, 2011.

_____. *Job and the Mystery of Suffering.* New York: Crossroads Books, 1996.

Rohr, Richard and John Feister. *Hope Against Darkness.* Cincinnati, OH: Saint Anthony Messenger Press, 2001.

Rosen, David. *Transforming Depression: Healing the Soul Through Creativity.* York Beach ME: Nicholas-Hays, Inc., 2002.

Scaer, David P. "The Concept of *Anfechtungen* in Luther's Thought." *Concordia Theological Quarterly* 47, no. 1, (January 1983): 15-30.

Scharmer, C. Otto. *Theory U: Leading from The Future as It Emerges.* Cambridge, MA: Society for Organizational Learning, 2007.

St John of the Cross. *Ascent of Mount Carmel.* (Translation by Allison Peers. Originally published by Westminster, MD: Newman Bookshop, 1946.) Minoela, NY: Dover Publications, 2008.

_____. *The Dark Night of the Soul.* Paul Negri & T.N.R. Rogers, editors. Mineola, NY: Dover Publications, 2003.

St Teresa of Avila. *Interior Castle.* (Translation by Allison Peers. Originally published by New York: Sheed & Ward, 1946.) Mineola, NY: Dover Publications, 1946.

Taylor, Barbara Brown. *Learning to Walk in the Dark.* New York: HarperOne, 2014.

The Cloud of Unknowing, translated by William Johnston. New York: Doubleday Image Books, 1973.

Tick, Edward. *War and the Soul.* Wheaton IL: Quest Books, 2005.

Tickle, Phyllis. *The Great Emergence, How Christianity is Changing and Why*. Grand Rapids, MI: Baker Books, 2008.

_____. *Emergence Christianity, What Is It, Where Is It Going, And Why It Matters*. Grand Rapids, MI: Baker Books, 2012.

Underhill, Evelyn. *Mysticism*. Santa Cruz, CA: (originally published in 1911) 2009.

Weems, Renita. *Listening for God*. New York: Touchstone Books, 1999.

Westerhoff, John. *Spiritual Life: The Foundation of Preaching and Teaching*, Louisville, KY: John Knox Press, 1994.

Wheatley, Margaret. *Finding Our Way, Leadership for an Uncertain Time*. San Francisco: Berrett-Koehler Publishers, 2004.

Wilbur, Ken. *A Brief History of Everything*. Boston: Shambhala, 2000.

_____. *Integral Spirituality: A Startling New Role for Religion in the Modern and Postmodern World*. Boston: Shambhala Publications. Kindle Edition.

Wink, Walter. *Engaging the Powers, Discernment and Resistance in a World of Domination*. Minneapolis: Fortress Press, 1992.

_____. *The Powers that Be*. New York: Random House, 1998.

Whyte, David. *The House of Belonging*. New York: Many Rivers Press, 1997.

_____. *Where Many Rivers Meet*. New York: Many Rivers Press, 1990.

Woodman, Mary Ann. "Dark Nights." *Presence*, Vol. 8(2), June 2002.

Wright, N. T., "Paul, Arabia and Elijah," originally published in *Journal of Biblical Literature*, 115:683–692. Accessed on line at http://ntwrightpage.com/Wright_Paul_Arabia_Elijah.pdf

Zagano, Phyllis, and Kevin Gillespie. "Embracing Darkness: A Theological and Psychological Study of Mother Teresa," *Spiritus: A Journal of Christian Spirituality*, Vol. 10(1), Spring 2010.

Appendix A
Clergy Survey – Questionnaire

The impetus for this survey comes from my Master's thesis at Andover Newton Theological School. The topic of that thesis is the transformative aspects of the dark night of the soul with a particular focus of how dark night experiences are perceived by and dealt with by those in ministry.

While there are those whose spiritual journey may never be interrupted by dark nights, and there may be those whose encounter with the dark night is so devastating that they recoil and leave their faith and/or their profession, the bulk of those in ministry, we may conjecture, fall somewhere between the two tails of the distribution, and have had some degree of encounter with the ebb and flow of their intimacy with God. Assuming that is true for you, I am contacting you to gather data and "stories" of those journeys into and through the dark night of the soul.

You do not need to be an expert on the dark night of the soul to participate. Your experience is your expertise. I am simply asking for some information on the nature, duration and frequency of those experiences as well as what you have found to be helpful techniques, relationships and resources in the journey. In order to assure confidentiality, you will not be asked for any personally identifying information, and all responses will be blinded so that no individual response can be linked with your information.

1. Please answer the following demographic questions

Age:

Gender affiliation:

Religious affiliation:

Ordained? Y/N

Years in ministry

Committed relationship status:

2. Please describe your most frequently used spiritual practice.

3. How often have you experienced what you might consider a dark night of the soul?

- Never (if never, please skip to the last question)
- Once
- Twice of three times
- Multiple times

4. How would you generally describe experience that marked the onset of your dark night(s)? (check all that apply)
(check all that apply)

☐ A crisis of faith

☐ Dryness in my spirituality

☐ A lack of any results of my previously held spiritual practice(s)

☐ Abandonment by God

☐ Lack of meaningful connection to God

☐ Temptation

☐ Loss of/ lack of spiritual director or advisor

☐ Personal suffering or innocent suffering of others

☐ Meaninglessness of theology

☐ God/The Divine seemed distant or nonexistent

☐ Not having a name of/for God

☐ Overwhelmed by unanswerable questions

☐ A sense of broken heart or heavy heart – it just all got too heavy

Other (please

specify) _____

5. Was there ever a precipitating event to your dark night(s)?
y/n (if yes, please describe)

6. How long did/does your dark night last?

○ How long did/does your dark night last? Relatively brief

○ A week or more but less than a month

○ Month(s) or more but less than a year

○ Sometimes more than a year

○ It is totally unpredictable and varied

7. Were there any particular issues that seemed more difficult or painful to deal with during the experience of your dark night(s)? Please explain:

8. What resources were most helpful during this time of spiritual darkness? (Check all that apply)

☐ Affirmations

☐ Continued prayer

☐ Meditation

☐ Ritual practices

☐ Holding onto some aspect of my faith

☐ Retreat, hermitage, or special events

☐ Significant personal relationship or group

☐ Spiritual director

☐ Other clergy or clergy group

☐ Reading(s) Bible or Specific book Please cite in "other"

Other (please specify readings)

9. How was your faith affected by the journey into and through the dark night of the soul?
Ultimately my faith has been strengthened by the experience

○ My faith has remained unchanged - I always held onto faith or the belief that God was "there"

○ My faith has become more fragile (something I must care for) as a result

○ My faith was somewhat altered or somehow lessened

○ I feel that my faith has slipped significantly as a result

Other (please specify)

10. What marked the end of the dark night experience(s)?

○ Nothing (I just woke up one day and it was gone)

○ Some type of conversion experience

○ Something clicked

○ A sense of deep change or transformation

○ A slow unfolding or opening

○ A sense of being touched by the Divine

Other (please specify)

11. How would you describe what changed in your spiritual life as a result of your dark night experiences?

12. How would you describe what changed in your spiritual practices as a result of your dark night experiences?

13. How has your perception of or experience of the Divine (or of God) changed as a result of your dark night experiences?

[blank box]

14. In what way has/have your previous dark night experience(s) prepared you or sensitized you for the possibility of any future dark night transitions?

[blank box]

15. What might you suggest to others going through this experience?

[blank box]

16. Insofar as it is possible to put into words, please write a brief description of your dark night experience(s).

[blank box]

17. Would you be willing to be interviewed about your experience?

Yes ○ No

Other (Contact information) [blank box]

Appendix B

Fowler's Stages of Faith

Fowler's Stages of Faith

- **Stage 0** – *Primal or Undifferentiated* faith (birth to 2 years) Fowler begins with this "pre-stage" which is characterized much like Piaget's early learning by the learning of the safety in one's environment. If nurturing is experienced consistently, one develops a sense of trust and safety about the world (which Fowler extrapolates to the Divine as well). Conversely, negative experiences cause one to develop distrust with the universe and the Divine. Transition to the next stage begins in learning thought and languages in speech and play.

- **Stage 1** – *Intuitive-Projective* faith (ages of three to seven), is characterized by a relative fluidity of thought patterns and the development of symbolic thought (that things may be representative of other thoughts or concepts). Religion is learned mainly through familial experiences, stories, images, and the people that one contacts.

- **Stage 2** – *Mythic-Literal* faith (in school-aged children), stage two children have a strong belief in the justice and reciprocity of the world (still rooted in a dualistic morality), and their deities are almost always anthropomorphic. During this time metaphors and symbolic language are still quite often misunderstood or are taken literally.

- **Stage 3** – *"Synthetic-Conventional"* faith (beginning in adolescence; ages 12 to adulthood) is characterized by a strong need for conformity to religious authority and the development of a personal identity either in alignment with that authority or in opposition to it. Any conflicts with one's beliefs are ignored or vilified at this stage due to the fear of threat from inconsistencies, including members of other conflicting belief sects.

- **Stage 4** – *"Individuative-Reflective"* faith (usually mid-twenties to late thirties) is a stage of angst and struggle. It is associated with the great drive for generativity in one's life. The individual takes personal responsibility for his or her beliefs and feelings. As one is able to reflect on one's own beliefs, one becomes open to a new complexity of faith, but this also increases the awareness of conflicts in one's belief.

- **Stage 5** – *"Conjunctive"* faith (mid-life crisis) acknowledges the paradox inherent in reality as well as in the symbols of moral systems. The individual resolves conflicts from previous stages by a complex understanding of a multidimensional, interdependent "truth" that is neither either/or but can only be expressed in a belief of "both… and."

- **Stage 6** – *"Universalizing"* faith, or what some might call "enlightenment." One treats any person with compassion. Because we are all born of a universality or communal world family, everyone should be treated with the universal principles of love and justice. Fowler sees very few people ever attaining this level of enlightenment and refers to them as "the saints."

Fowler's Stages of Faith[226]

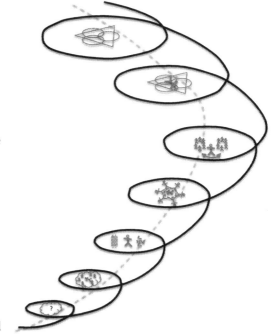

Stage 6
Universalizing

Stage 5
Conjunctive

Stage 4
Individuative-Reflective

Stage 3
Synthetic-Conventional

Stage 2
Mythic-Literal

Stage 1
Intuitive-Projective

Stage 0
Primal-Undifferentiated

---

[226] Fowler, *Stages*, 275 (adapted).

Appendix C

Resources

Audio Recordings

Bache, Christopher. *Dark Night of the Species Soul*. IONS Lecture, 2001. http://www.noetic.org/library/audio-lectures/chris-bache-dark-night-species-soul/

Borysenko, Joan. *Meditations on Courage and Compassion*: Developing Resilience in Turbulent Times. Hay House Recordings. 2010.

Myss, Carolyn. *Spiritual Madness*. Sounds True Recordings, 2002.

Various CDs by Richard Rohr. Available from CAC.org bookstore http://store.cac.org/CDs_c_13.html. Especially recommended are: *Falling Upward, Soul Centering Through Nature, The Art of Letting Go,* and *Men & Grief.*

Weiss, Brian. *Spiritual Progress Through Regression*. Hay House Recordings, 2008.

Music: Most of the participants in the survey reported using music as a tool for centering, for grounding and for bringing back a connection to life. Your own choices will come though many may already be recorded in your soul as the vehicles of the dark night.

Books

Ackerman, John. *Listening to God*. Minneapolis: Alban Institute, 2001.

Beckham, Betsy and Christine Valtners Painter. *Awakening the Creative Spirit: Bringing the Arts to Spiritual Direction*. Harrisburg, PA: Morehouse Publishing, 2010.

Benner, David. *Spirituality and the Awakening Self: the Sacred Journey of Transformation*. Grand Rapids: Brazos Press, 2012.

Bonhoeffer, Deitrich. *Life Together: the Exploration of Faith in Community*. New York: HarperOne, 2009.

_____. *The Cost of Discipleship*. New York: Touchstone, 1995.

Borysenko, Joan. *Minding the Body, Mending the Mind*. Cambridge, MA: DeCapo Press. 2007.

_____. *Pocketful of Miracles: Prayers, Meditations and Affirmations to Nurture Your Spirit Every Day of the Year*. New York: Warner Books, 1994.

Chodron, Pema. *When Things Fall Apart, Heart Advice for Difficult Times*. Boston: Shambhala, 2002.

Delio, Ilia. *Christ in Evolution*. (Maryknll, NY: Orbis Books, 2008) eBook

Finley, James, *Merton's Palace of Nowhere*, Notre Dame, IN: Notre Dame Press, 1978.

Gawain, Shakti. *The Four Levels of Healing: Balancing Spiritual, Mental, Emotional and Spiritual Aspects of Life.* Novato, CA: Nataraj Publishing, 1997.

Hanh, Thich Nhat. *Living Buddha, Living Christ* (10th Anniversary Edition). New York: Berkeley Publishing Group, 2007

_____. *Reconciliation: Healing the Inner Child.* Berkeley, CA: Parallax Press, 2010.

_____. *True Love: A Practice for Awakening the Heart.* Boston: Shambala Publications, 1997.

Holmes, Barbara. *Joy Unspeakable, Contemplative Practices of the Black Church.* Minneapolis, MN: Augsburg Press, 2004.

Johnston William. *Mystical Theology: The Science of Love.* Maryknoll, NY: Orbis Books, 1996.

Kidd, Sue Monk. *When the Heart Waits: Spiritual Direction for Life's Sacred Questions.* New York: HarperCollins, 1990.

Kushner, Harold. *The Book of Job, When Bad Things Happen To A Good Person.* New York: Schocken Books/Random House, 2012.

May, Gerald. *The Dark Night of the Soul.* San Francisco: HarperCollins Publishers, 2004.

_____. *The Wisdom of Wilderness, Experiencing the Healing Power of Nature.* New York: HarperCollins e-books, 2007.

McCall, Morgan, Mike Lombardo & Ann Morrison. *The Lessons of Experience.*

Merton, Thomas. *The Wisdom of the Desert.* New York: Abbey of Gethsemane, New Directions Press, 1960.

_____. *New Seeds of Contemplation.* New York: New Directions Books, 1961.

Moore, Thomas. *Dark Nights of the Soul, A guide to Finding Your Way Through Life's Ordeals.* New York: Gotham Books, 2004.

Rohr, Richard. *Everything Belongs: The Gift of Contemplative Prayer.* New York: Crossroad Publications, 2003.

_____. *Things Hidden.* Cincinnati, OH: Saint Anthony Messenger Press, 2008.

_____. *The Naked Now: Learning to See as the Mystics See.* New York: Crossroads Publishing Co., 2009.

_____. *Breathing Under Water.* Cincinnati, OH: St. Anthony Messenger Press, 2011.

Rosen, David. *Transforming Depression: Healing the Soul Through Creativity.* York Beach ME: Nicholas-Hays, Inc., 2002.

Rumi, Jalal al-Din. *The Essential Rumi* (edited by Coleman Barks). New York: HarperCollins, 1995.

Stringfellow, William. *A Private and Public Faith*. Eugene, OR: Wipf and Stock, 1999.

_____. *Essential Writings* (edited by Bill Wylie-Kellerman). Maryknoll, NY: Orbis Books, 2013.

_____. *Free In Obedience*. Eugene, OR: Wipf and Stock, 2006.

Taylor, Barbara Brown. *Learning to Walk in the Dark*. New York: HarperOne, 2014.

Weems, Renita. *Listening for God*. New York: Touchstone Books, 1999.

Wheatley, Margaret. *Finding Our Way, Leadership for an Uncertain Time*. San Francisco: Berrett-Koehler Publishers, 2004.

Made in the USA
Columbia, SC
29 November 2017